A DIRECTORS GUILD OF AMERICA BOOK

SHELDON LEONARD

AND THE SHOW GOES ON

BROADWAY AND HOLLYWOOD ADVENTURES

FOREWORD BY
ANDY GRIFFITH

LIMELIGHT EDITIONS
LE
Books of the Performing Arts

To My Wife Frankie

First Limelight Edition February 1995

Copyright © 1994 by Sheldon Leonard
All rights reserved under International and Pan-American Copyright Conventions.
Published in the United States by Proscenium Inc., New York, and simultaneously in
Canada by Fitzhenry & Whiteside, Limited, Toronto.

Library of Congress Cataloging-in-Publication Data
Leonard, Sheldon, 1907-
And the show goes on : Broadway and Hollywood adventures / by Sheldon Leonard ; with
a foreword by Andy Griffith. — 1st Limelight ed.
p.   cm.
Includes index.
ISBN 0-87910-184-9
1. Leonard, Sheldon, 1907- . 2. Television producers and directors—United States—
Biography. 3. Actors—United States—Biography.   I. Title.
PN1992.4.L383A3 1995
791.45′023′092—dc20
[B]   94-40934
                                                                CIP

Table of Contents

Photo inserts follow pages 70 and 134.

Author's Note

I never kept a diary. Consequently, I had to rely on memory when I undertook to record things that happened up to sixty years ago. My aging memory served me well except when it came to dates or names. For instance, I couldn't remember which of Bill Cosby's children was his first born. All five of his children have names beginning with E. It's confusing. So, when I got to the point in this book where I tell about how I kept him prisoner in a hotel room seven thousand miles away, while his first child was getting itself born, I took refuge in vagueness.

It's true that I could have called him and asked him for the name of his first born, but it's hard to get him on the phone and, besides, it isn't important.

Likewise, when it comes to dates, I'll guarantee them, give or take a couple of years either way, but I can't do better than that. However, I can guarantee the accuracy of whatever memorabilia you will encounter in these pages.

I think I can claim that on a scale of 10 for accuracy, I've earned a 9.5.

With the passing of the years, and the human tendency to romanticize the bygone days, a 9.5 grade, even when self-proclaimed, is — I trust you'll agree — pretty damn good. But, then, I've been held to a high standard by my editor, Ira Skutch, whose expert assistance has been invaluable to me.

S.L.

1959 — I was on Broadway in half a hit called *Destry*. What I mean by half a hit is, we stayed open — just barely. Monday through Thursday we were on twofers — two tickets for the price of one — and on holidays — Thanksgiving, Christmas, and the like — there was a sign out front that said, "Matinee Today."

I was at a kind of low point for me. I had pretty well struck out in motion pictures, I was in a musical that was barely open, and I didn't want to go back to nightclubs. So I told Abe Lastfogel, then head of William Morris, that I would like to try TV. It seemed the only thing left.

I was told that a man named Sheldon Leonard would come to see me one night and come backstage. A little time went by and I didn't think much more about it. And one night, after the show and curtain calls — which didn't take very long — I passed the stage door on my way to my dressing room. There was a man standing there smiling. I kind of smiled back and went on. I thought I had seen him before — maybe playing "heavies" in movies. So I went next door to Art Lund's dressing room and asked, "Who is that guy at the stage door?"

Art said, "Sheldon Leonard."

Well, it didn't take a heartbeat to get back down there. I didn't know the wonderful future that was ahead of me by this fine man coming to New York to see me.

We talked that night and some of the next day about his notion of a show for me. To tell you the truth, I really didn't care for the notion, but I did like him. The idea was that I would be the sheriff of a small town down south (where else?) and also the justice of the peace and editor of the paper.

And, I would tell funny stories about the people who lived in this little town of —"Mayberry." I would be a widower with a small son.

He went home to Los Angeles, and a few weeks later I asked him to come back to be sure I heard it all right. Well, I still wasn't sure of the idea, but I still liked him. We shook hands and agreed to do it. We shot it in January of 1960 as a spin-off from *Danny Thomas*, and it was a big hit and sold right away.

Sheldon is extraordinarily bright — a fine producer — writer — actor — and director. He has an amzing ability to put people together who will work well together — on our show, Aaron Ruben, Bob Sweeney, and me. And when Don Knotts called to say he would like to be on the show, Sheldon hired him, and that turned the whole thing around.

We read two scripts each Thursday — gave notes on the first one, and worked on the second one the rest of the day. After we had read each script, Sheldon would say what he thought — what was good, bad, how to fix it. Then he would leave. After all, he was executive producer on just about every show on the lot. He had quite a lot to do.

Sometimes we would go Sheldon's way with our rewrites — sometimes we wouldn't. He never argued with us — ego never entered into it. He only wanted what worked best for the show and for us. That's another example of his knowledge and his selflessness — he did not set down solid rules for our show. He allowed it and us to evolve into what we became.

The things I was troubled by were my many jobs — sheriff, justice of the peace, editor of the paper, telling funny stories about the people who lived in "Mayberry." We lost the editor of the paper right away — pretty soon after, the justice of the peace. And when Don Knotts came along, we all knew that he should be funny and I should play straight for him. So, I told fewer and fewer stories about people in

viii

"Mayberry." Then, over the years, my character was straight for the many fine comic actors we had — Floyd the Barber — Goober — The Darling Family — Earnest T. Bass — Otis the Town Drunk — even Helen the Girlfriend — Aunt Bea — and Opie.

Sheldon allowed all these changes and helped them to happen through our years — no fighting — no pain. You don't often find that in our business.

So, the man who was at the stage door that night at *Destry* gave me my best and happiest working years and became my friend for life — Sheldon Leonard.

Andy Griffith
Manteo, North Carolina
March 16, 1994

My parents were lower middle-class Jews.

My mother's maiden name was Anna Levitt. Her father, my grandfather, had been a scribe in the court of Czar Nicholas, a position of some prestige since, in those days, the ability to read and write was limited to an elite few. He lost his job in one of the periodic anti-Semitic purges. He came to America with no skills except the ability to read and write, skills that were not as salable in America as they had been in semi-medieval Russia.

At age twelve, my mother, the oldest of eight siblings, went to work in a sweatshop to support the family. Eventually, she saved enough money to buy a pushcart for her father, the ex-scribe.

My father, Frank Bershad, was a salesman. Not a salesman of staples. He preferred gimmicks. At one time or another, he sold flexible watch bands, Swedish fruit juicers, electric mouse traps, frozen crab meat, etc. He firmly believed that the gadget that would make his fortune was almost within reach. His ship was about to come in — although right now it was just over the horizon.

He married my mother when he was nineteen and she was twenty-one. I was born in New York City on Washington's birthday, February 22, 1907.

I spent my pre-teen years in the streets of the south Bronx, a wonderful place for growing up. There was practically no automobile traffic in those pre-World War I days, so the streets were available for roller skating, bicycling, stick ball, Simon says, and other diversions.

We were an eclectic gang of kids — Jews, Italians, Poles, Germans and what-have-you. A normal form of address was, "Hey, you dago bastard...." For which the appropriate response was, "Whadda ya want, you kike prick?"

Such terms of endearment carried no hatred. They were our substitute for an adequate vocabulary, and no one took offense at them. Consequently, I was unprepared for what I ran into when my parents moved me and my younger brother, Alfred, to suburban Belleville, New Jersey.

We moved into a modest house on Malone Avenue in June of 1919. It was not my element. The ambiance was very waspy and I was a kid from the streets of south Bronx. I made no friends. I spent most of July and August in a boy scout camp, where I rose to the level of Eagle Scout.

School started in mid-September. P.S. 3 was a ten-minute walk from our house. On the first day of school, I made that short walk eagerly, anticipating the chance to meet other kids, to make friends.

I merged with the milling mob of kids who were responding to the teachers' shouted directions:

"Everybody on the playground!"

"Boys on the left. Girls on the right."

"Size places! Size places!"

I was a big kid. I squeezed myself in between two boys at the end of the line. The boy on my right snarled, "Get away from me! You smell from herring!"

What was he talking about? How could I smell of herring? I didn't eat herring. I didn't like herring. The kid was crazy.

The kid on my left, who I would later come to know as Bill Traphagen, made things clear. "Get away from me, Jew Boy!" he commanded. "I don't like kikes!"

It was my first encounter with anti-Semitism, and it was just the beginning. A gang of kids, led by Bill Traphagen, would wait for me after school to mock me and deride me. I took to exiting from the school by the back door. I'd make my way home through side streets and huddle in my room, bewildered and shamed.

One day, they caught on to my use of the back door, and surrounded me when I came out. After a minute or two of ritual taunting Kikey Ikey, Abie, Kosher Kid, Bill Traphagen introduced a new gambit. "Do you like that tie he's wearing?" he asked the smallest kid in the group.

The kid, taken aback, responded with a positive nod.

"Then help yourself. Take it," Bill instructed. "He won't stop you."

Timidly, the kid advanced.

Somewhere, in another dimension, there was the sound of a camel's back breaking under this final straw.

"No!" I snarled, while adrenalin bubbled through my bloodstream. "You take it, Bill."

He had no choice. He was surrounded by his acolytes. His hesitation was momentary. He came toward me. He reached for my tie, and I belted him in the mouth.

I beat the crap out fof Bill Traphagen!

Oh! It felt so good!

I kept hitting him, even after he yelled "Uncle," which was a serious breach of schoolyard ethics. But oh! It felt so good.

Over the next few months, I adjusted to the ostracism by becoming a bully. I beat up on whoever called me names.

Although this approach didn't make friends for me, it gained me respect and, eventually, freedom from abuse, but I was a lonely kid. I took refuge in books. I read incessantly — Horatio Alger, Henty, Dickens, Conan Doyle, anything in print. My imagination, fed by the mass of literary images, flourished. I didn't merely read about Tarzan in the jungle, I was there with him, swinging from tree to tree.

I didn't know it then, but I was laying the foundation for a career in the world of imagination — the entertainment world.

When I was fourteen, my family moved out of Belleville, back to New York. I entered Stuyvesant High School in lower Manhattan and promptly immersed myself in sports. If I wasn't sweating, I wasn't enjoying myself. Joe Bromberger changed that.

We met in high school, and, for whatever reason, became buddies. He, more than anyone else, would determine the path my life was to take. Joe had a rheumatic heart. His extracurricular world was the Literary Society, the Bibliophiles, and the Dramatic Society. Since Joe couldn't share my athletic activities, and because he was my buddy, I joined the Literary Society, the Bibliophiles, and, significantly, the Dramatic Society.

Still in his teens, Joe had already set his sights on a career as an actor. He tried out for all the Dramatic Society's productions and I dragged along.

Joe had talent. As we trudged through the high school years, he shone in a variety of productions, and, with the help of a pretty good director, Gustav Blum, of the English department, I did well, too. More importantly, I liked it.

Gus Blum had been a director in the Yiddish theatre before he abandoned it for the security of a teaching job, but he left his heart behind the footlights. Some of his deep affection for show business rubbed off on me.

Joe introduced me to Gray's Drug Store on Broadway at the corner of 43rd St., a scant twenty-minute walk from Stuyvesant. Gray's was an ordinary drug store on the ground level and an extraordinary theatre ticket agency in the basement. If a current Broadway production had unsold seats shortly before curtain time, they were sent over to Gray's basement where they were put on sale at half price. Joe and I became matinée hounds.

Broadway productions had two matinées a week, one on Saturday and a second on Wednesday or Thursday. That meant we could see as many as three shows a week at fifty-five cents a shot for a pretty good seat in the second balcony.

We gorged ourselves on theatre.

Inevitably, so much exposure kindled in me a growing enthusiasm for acting. Soon I was trying out for the school plays because I liked doing them and not just because of Joe.

In my senior year in Stuyvesant, the football team, on which I was the right guard, played Erasmus Hall High School for the Municipal Championship. We won the game, six to three, and I won something much more important. I got to meet a little blonde cheerleader for Erasmus, Frankie Bober, with whom I was to share my life up to the present day.

When I went on to Syracuse University, I continued my thespian activities under the eyes of a brilliant coach. Sawyer Falk, the head of the Performing Arts department of the School of Speech at Syracuse, had a unique directing style. Professor Falk would sit quietly in the auditorium making notes, as an actor developed his performance through days of rehearsal.

After five or six rehearsal days, he would assemble his actors and go to work on them. If there was a shred of dishonest theatricality in your performance, he would spot it. He would tear your work apart, then put it together again. He was brutal and he was gentle. I was lucky to have been under his influence. We became good friends.

June, 1929, I doffed my cap and gown, brought my diploma to the framer, and took up my responsibilities as head counselor at Camp Wakitan in the Ramapo Mountains of upper New York State. I had worked there, in various capacities, throughout my college summers. The camp, beautifully located on Lake Stahahe, midway between Tuxedo Park and Bear Mountain, was maintained by the Hebrew Orphan Asylum of New York. The orphanage had a second camp, for girls, on an adjacent lake. The four hundred girls and five hundred boys sheltered at the institution were sent to camp in three age sets. The six-to-tens in June, eleven-to-fourteens in July, and fifteen-to-seventeens in August.

I had spent my summers there as a volunteer, first as a swimming counselor, and later as the head counselor. The surrounding mountains were full of wild life — deer, racoons, foxes, and snakes. In my spare time I would pick up my forked stick and a burlap bag to scout the surrounding wilderness for copperheads and timber rattlers, which I sold to Dr. Raymond Ditmars of the Bronx Zoo for a dollar a foot. They were milked for their venom, which was used to produce anti-venom.

The summer of '29 ended.We boarded up the cabins, stored the canoes on racks, deflated the footballs and basketballs, boxed the baseball equipment and the handballs, and put the camp to sleep for the winter. It was time for me to start my career. I was in no hurry to take up the job which had been set for me by one of the Syracuse alumni. I was to be an apprentice customer's man with the brokerage firm of Bauerdorf and Company, at 26 Broadway, starting with a salary appropriate for a young man who was about to get married.

I delayed going to work as a broker because I loved working with the H.O.A. kids. They were deeply appreciative of adult companionship. They were not all orphans, as in many cases they came to the institution from broken homes.

Whatever the reason, these kids were highly motivated. Maybe the absence of parental concern made them eager for adult approval. Maybe the close quarters of institutional life stimulated competitiveness. Certainly the knowledge that excellence was the key to a better life style was a powerful motivating force. An exceptional percentage of those kids turned out to be high achievers in the professions, in business, and in government. Now, some sixty years later, many of them still keep in touch with me.

At the end of the camp season in the summer of '29, Frankie and I decided I should stop fooling around. With marriage impending, it was time for me to start my career as a stockbroker.

My timing wasn't good.

On that morning in October of '29, minutes before the market opened at ten a.m., a junior executive of the firm of Bauerdorf and Company was getting me started. He showed me where the men's room was and where to hang my hat. Then he took me to the glass-domed ticker tape machine. "And here is the booklet that gives you all the symbols. 'X' stands for U. S. Steel. 'GM' is General Motors, and so on. The numbers on the tape stand for the price of the transaction and the number of shares. For instance, here you've got a block of ten thousand shares of Dow Chemical.....Wow! Somebody must be unloading. It's off six points.....Now, here's TWA.....What's going on here?.....and General Motors.....What the hell!....Excuse me. I gotta go. We'll finish up later."

He never did finish up. The catastrophic market crash of '29 was underway. It precipitated the Depression of the thirties. In just a few weeks Bauerdorf and Company was out of business, and I was out on the street.

However, my performance as a stock broker was not a total loss. In its few weeks duration I had sold my friend Eddie Carter a hundred shares of Irving Trust at five and my fiancee fifty shares of Phillips Petroleum at six.

I borrowed four thousand dollars from my father and bought a one-third interest in my Uncle Lew's millinery

business. He made expensive hats. The time was the early
thirties. The Depression was gathering momentum. Expensive hats were not a priority item.

How about my timing?

Stevedoring on the White Star Line docks and life
guarding at Luna Park in Coney Island followed in quick
succession. In the summer of 1930, at Manhattan Beach, I ran
into a high school buddy. Back in school days, Bob Weitman
had given me boxing lessons. To my surprise, he hadn't
chosen a career as a prize fighter, for which he had a marked
aptitude, as the bruises on my jaw could attest. He had
applied for the Paramount Theatre circuit's training school
for assistant theatre managers, had completed the course,
and was now the manager of the prestigious Brooklyn
Paramount Theatre. Wowie! That was for me.

Bob gave me an introduction to the managers of the
training school and they accepted me. I went through a
three-month course learning how to mix a cleaning solution
for mopping a theatre's marble floors, how to operate the air
conditioning system, how to reload the toilet paper contain-
ers in the rest rooms, and, incidentally, how to analyze a
motion picture for promotional purposes.

I didn't realize it then, but I had just dipped my toes
into show business.

When I finished the course, I was sent to the Eastman
Theatre in Rochester, as assistant manager. The theatre had
been built by George Eastman, as a civic gesture. It had floors
of imported Italian marble, original Maxfield Parrish wall
murals, bronze poster frames from Tiffany, deep pile carpets,
and it did lousy business.

I fell into a routine in Rochester. As a theatre manager,
I lived an upside-down life. When the theatre closed, after
two a.m., it was too late for a meal in a regular restaurant.
The only place open was the roadhouse on the outskirts of

town that served food at all hours — along with illegal booze, of which Rochester had an abundant supply.

In prohibition days, Rochester was an important point on the route for booze being smuggled down from Canada. The people involved in that cottage industry patronized the same roadhouse that had become my after-work hangout. I made interesting friends, many of whom had bent noses and thick ears. They had girl friends who didn't have bent noses or thick ears, although they were likely to be pleasantly thick in other places. One of them loved movies, so we spent many pleasant evenings discussing the movies she liked, and other things.

One night, in the winter of 1930, I walked back to my hotel after a late screening. It was bitterly cold. As I approached the entrance to the hotel, slipping and sliding on the snow-covered sidewalk, two men, who had been loitering by the entrance, approached me.

"You the guy from the Eastman Theatre?" one of them asked. I nodded, and he belted me a good one, right between the eyes. They went to work on me.

The only thing that saved me from a severe beating was the icy pavement. The two thugs couldn't get a secure footing from which to tee off on me. They did the best they could and took off, leaving me with world-class shiners on both eyes.

The next day, I skulked in my office, not choosing to display my redesigned eyes in the theatre lobby. That was the day two detectives from the Rochester police force chose to visit me. It was management's custom to supply members of the force with passes to the theatre. That assured cooperation from the police department in such matters as encroaching on the sidewalk with our posters, or blocking nearby entrances with our holding crowds. However, lest they forget that they owed us, they had to come to my office once a month to pick up their passes and say, "Thank you."

These two guys came into my office, took one look at my black eyes, and burst into hearty laughter. "I see that Rocky caught up with you," said one.

Rocky was Rocco Lorenzo, the mob's chief representative in charge of operations between Canada and New York. It seemed that the girl who liked movies was his property, and last night's episode was his way of telling me so.

By the time my eyes regained their natural color, the Eastman Theatre — succumbing to the continuing Depression and a string of bad pictures — closed its doors, and I, with little regret, went back to New York to resume job-hunting.

Frankie and I were married in 1931. She was twenty-three, and I was twenty-four. Our wedding was a gloomy affair. My mother had recently died; Frankie's grandfather, too, had died a short time earlier. Under the circumstances, it seemed inappropriate to conduct an elaborate ceremony, but Frankie's parents, in anticipation of a couple of hundred guests, had already hired the enormous ballroom of the St. George Hotel in Brooklyn for the affair. So, the nuptials took place in that cavernous room with Frankie in her wedding gown, me in my tuxedo, and with Frankie's brother, mother, and father, and my brother and father the only witnesses.

Surely a marriage begun under such circumstances was doomed. To make things worse, Frankie was headed for the security of teaching high school biology, while I was drifting about in the uncertain world of the Theatre. An obvious mismatch. Besides, everybody knows that show business marriages don't last.

Recently, on the occasion of our sixtieth anniversary, Frankie and I reflected on our folly.

Early in 1932, I was indulging my newly-developed hobby — walking the streets. In front of the Guild Theatre I ran into a couple of dozen unkempt, haphazardly-garbed young people who were busy making theatrical history.

They were young actors who had just been put out on the street when The Theatre Guild dissolved the apprentice program of which they had been a part. Now they were coming to the conclusion that they didn't need The Theatre Guild. Amongst them were playwrights, directors, actors, and all sorts of assorted talents. They were self-sufficient. They would stay together.

Over the next several years they would stage plays like *Men in White, Golden Boy, Awake and Sing,* and many others. They would give us writers like Clifford Odets, directors like Elia Kazan, Harold Clurman, and Lee Strasberg, actors like Franchot Tone, John Garfield, and Lee Cobb. They would call themselves The Group Theatre.

But on that day in 1932 they were just a ragged band of hopefuls. Among them were Bobby Lewis, Sandy Meisner, Tony Kraber, and my classmate at Stuyvesant High School, J. Edward Bromberg, known to me as Joe Bromberger, the guy who was responsible for my involvement in acting.

A serendipitous reunion. Joe and I embraced; and there was a brief exchange of resumes. Joe had gotten married since last we met, and so had I. He was out of a job and so was I. But he had an inkling of what his next job was to be, and I had none.

He was going to a resort hotel in New England with the people who were to become The Group Theatre. There, they were to be the resident entertainment source. I was going to continue walking the streets in search of a job.

"I don't get it," Joe said. "You are a good actor. Instead of looking for a job doing things you do badly, like selling millinery or tossing baggage on the docks, why don't you look for a job doing what you do well? Acting."

"Oh, come on! I can get by in amateur productions, but on a professional level? No chance."

"Trust me. I've been in and around the professional theatre for four years now. You're as good as you have to be to get started. Besides, the country is in a Depression. Jobs are hard to find. Almost impossible. But the theatre doesn't feel the Depression. As a matter of fact, depressions are good for the entertainment trades. People go to the theatre to escape."

"I wouldn't know how to go about getting an acting job."

"It's just like selling magazine subscriptions door to door. If you ring enough bells, sooner or later you'll make a sale. Like if you open enough oysters, sooner or later you'll find a pearl."

"Okay. Where do I find the oysters?"

—

two

Curtain Up!

The theatre of the thirties was about to become the focus of my professional life for the next ten years. It was quite different from the theatre as we know it today. It was more vigorous, more self sufficient, and very much more glamorous. Women didn't go to a Broadway show in slacks; they probably wore cocktail dresses. Men wore black tie — not the snap-on type. In those days they knew how to tie them, a skill that will certainly have disappeared by the time the next generation comes along. We didn't know it then, but the Great White way was in the process of becoming the Sleazy White Way. Happily, I couldn't foresee the decline of the theatre. For me it was glamorous, full of promise, and, above all, exciting.

The oyster beds toward which Joe directed me were Zolotow's column in the *New York Times*, the bulletin board at the Actor's Equity Association, and certain information services where, for a small fee, you were given access to all the theatrical publications — *Billboard, Variety*, etc., as well as a tip sheet of rumor, speculation, and occasional fact as to where production activity was occurring.

I started opening oysters wherever my information sources suspected there was something happening. I learned how actors job hunted. You heard that producer so-and-so had optioned a play, so you went to the indicated address, looked up the office number on the lobby directory, took the elevator to the proper office, approached the secretary-receptionist, oozing charm, and asked, "Doing any casting?"

Usually, the answer was "No." Occasionally you got a "Yes," followed by a curt "but there's nothing in it for you."

The only open parts were for teenage albinos. Once in a blue moon, if you weren't too young or too old, too tall or too short, too Jewish or too gentile, you got a chance to read for a part.

That happened to me in the early fall of '32. I got to read. The producer, Brock Pemberton, liked my reading. He asked me what I had done professionally. Joe had prepared me for that question. "Make up a list of out-of-town jobs. Nobody is going to check up on you," he said.

So my answer was, "I had two years with the Jessie Bonstell Repertory Company in Detroit, playing heavies and second leads. I was with Cukor Kondolf in stock in Rochester for a year, then I did a year and a half with the Chicago company of *Abie's Irish Rose*."

Mr. Pemberton was still smiling. Wow! So far so good.

"Okay. What's your salary?"

Joe had not prepared me for that. In the theatre of the thirties you seldom negotiated your salary, unless you were stepping up in the size and importance of the part, or unless you had a solid success behind you. You were a hundred-and-fifty-dollar actor, a two-hundred-dollar actor, or, if you were blazing hot, a three-hundred-dollar guy. Bearing in mind that fourteen dollars a week was an attractive salary in those Depression days, three-digit salaries might seem exotic, but the chances were that you would work very few weeks, or none at all, in a season, so you had to latch on to an occasional long run in order to survive.

As I said, Joe hadn't prepared me for this. Remembering that twenty dollars a week was a salary to be envied in the real world, and not wanting to pin too cheap a price tag on myself lest I lose the producer's respect, I said, "Well, sir, my established salary is twenty-five dollars a week."

The established Equity minimum was forty dollars.

The interview was over.

But, like the man said, if you open enough oysters..... With just three hundred and forty dollars in our bank account, I landed a part in a play called *Hotel Alimony*. It was about the New York State law that stipulated that if you fell behind in your alimony payments you went to jail until you got caught up. Nobody has ever explained how you got caught up on your alimony while you were in jail. At any rate, that's what the play was about.

Most shows played a couple of weeks or more out of town before opening on Broadway. That gave the writers and directors a chance to evaluate the audience reaction and make revisions before the New York opening. Boston, Washington, New Haven, and Princeton were popular break-in towns. In this case, for whatever reason, we were going to open cold at the Royale Theatre on 45th St. in New York.

For me it was the dawning of a career. I was about to set foot on the path that I was to follow for more than half a century. I was about to face the awesome array of critics who could determine, not merely my well-being in terms of a prosperous engagement, but my career and, thereby, my life.

The ogres would be out there in a sea of white shirt fronts and decolletage —among them Brooks Atkinson of *The New York Times*, and John Mason Brown of *The Herald Tribune*, who had just destroyed a pretty good play by starting his review with the statement that he had "...seen the play under unfavorable circumstances. The curtain was up." Walter Winchell would be present, and, perhaps, Dorothy Parker, who had said of Katharine Hepburn in *The Lake*, "She ran the gamut of emotions from A to B."

If a play got a good notice from Atkinson or Brown, it was a good bet that it would settle in for a long run. The day after the favorable reviews appeared there would be lines around the block at the box office. Get bad reviews, and you could start composing the closing notice.

Opening night at the Royale Theatre.

It was nail-biting time backstage. Careers were about to be made or destroyed. The seasoned pros knew that we might be mounting the tumbrels. They huddled behind the sets and spoke in whispers. The stage manager called "Fifteen minutes." Then "Ten minutes." "Five." And, finally, "Curtain going up!"

Why was everybody so nervous? What was there to be afraid of? I wasn't afraid. The adrenalin was flowing. I was a mile high. I was going to be a smash. They were going to love me like they did at college. Hadn't the critic for *The Syracuse Herald* described my performance as Ferdinand DeLevis in Galsworthy's *Loyalties* as "...well above professional standards"? Didn't I get three curtain calls after my performance as Pastor Manders in Ibsen's *Ghosts*? How about the stream of congratulations back at the fraternity house for my role as the big brother in Eugene O'Neill's *Beyond the Horizon*? Audiences loved me. I couldn't wait to get on stage so they could enjoy me.

A hush settled over the audience as the footlights came on. The curtain rose and the actors on stage spoke the first lines of dialogue. We were underway! There was occasional laughter from out front. I straightened my necktie, and checked my fly. Finally, ten minutes deep in the first act, my cue came. I strode on stage with all the assurance of ignorance.

There is nothing so valuable for an actor, particularly in comedy, as self-assurance. Even if, as in my case, it is unjustified.

Don't ask me for scientific proof, but every performer knows, empirically, that the members of an audience can smell fear. Flop sweat. On the other hand, they immediately recognize confidence. It is reassuring. They warm to it. My arrogant self-assurance did a couple of good things — it enabled me to be relaxed and at ease on stage, and it put the audience on my side, so that when I came to my first comedy line I got a much bigger laugh than the line deserved. The laugh trailed off into applause.

Although I had a wealth of amateur acting experience behind me, under the supervision of excellent coaches, none of it had been with comedy. Consequently the audience reaction staggered me. I lost my next line of dialogue in the laugh, a class A sin in comedy acting. Then, trying to recover, I waited too long to speak again, thus leaving a gaping hole in the dialogue.

Forty-six seconds after starting my career as a professional actor, I was hit by stage fright. I became preoccupied with controlling the tremor in my voice to the exclusion of anything else. I went on automatic pilot, and that saved me. Without conscious thought, I performed the lines and business that had been stored in my brain by weeks of rehearsal, while my conscious mind concentrated on the problem of concealing the trembling of my voice and my kneecaps. Somehow I got through the balance of the play creditably. Somebody up there liked me.

According to tradition, after the opening night performance the entire company retreated to Sardi's restaurant to wait for the early edition of the morning newspapers and the reviews. There was much brave talk. One actor's wife had spoken with Kelcey Allen of *Women's Wear Daily* between the second and third acts, and he said he liked it. The stage manager had stopwatched the laughs, and we got almost two minutes more than the comedy hit, *Dulcy*. And didn't we get four curtain calls? Granted that the stage manager had milked the last two, but it was still pretty good.

In my opinion there are few things that men do, with the possible exception of a moon landing, that carry with it the emotional highs of a successful Broadway show opening. For months thereafter you stride through life and your feet never touch the ground. For a long time after the opening, when the curtain comes down your dressing room becomes a meeting place for friends, admirers, autograph seekers, and theatrical agents. It's wonderful.

From the actor's point of view the financial benefits that result from a hit are less important than the career enhancement. There's something for everyone: salary increases, picture offers, endorsements, and other goodies.

Naturally, the disappointment that goes with a flop is equally severe. Months of concentrated work and hope go down the drain in a few grim hours.

Hotel Alimony had opened; the critics had written their reviews; and now the presses were rolling. Gathered in Sardi's, the cast waited. Our fate hung in the balance. Someone was assigned to stand by the Times Square newsstand and seize the papers as soon as they were unloaded from the truck. He needn't have been in such a hurry. The critics murdered us.

There wasn't a single quote to use in the ads. Burns Mantle wrote, "Out of an inherent sense of decency I was tempted to ignore *Hotel Alimony* as though it had never happened. Reviewing it is a dirty job, but someone has to do it."

Hotel Alimony closed after six performances, but I came out of it smelling like a rose. Agents, directors, and producers had been among the first nighters; and I hadn't done too badly. The reviews had let me down gently with adjectives like "competent," "vigorous," "refreshing," and the like — and I was a new face.

In the weeks after the closing I had several nibbles. I settled for the prospect that promised the most immediate money. I signed to go to the island of Jamaica to play the heavy in a "British quota picture" called *Drums in the Night*. I was guaranteed six weeks at four-fifty a week. A positive bonanza!

At that time, the British had established a quota for the importation of American-made films. They would accept five American productions for each British film that American distributors bought. The flaw in the arrangement was that the British simply were not making enough films. We wanted to sell them hundreds, and they could only offer us dozens. Naturally, if they couldn't make enough pictures to satisfy our needs, we'd help them. American producers would make pictures on British soil, with British personnel, and sell them back to themselves so that they could unload five of the American films for each of the ones they bought. Hence the "British Quota Film."

The *Drums in the Night* company sailed from New York in a ship of the United Fruit Lines' "Great White Fleet." In spite of its pretentious label, our ship was a banana boat. The Caribbean islands were, as yet, unexploited except as a source of tropical produce and rum. They were decades away from the days when they would become glamorous resorts. The fruit boats were the only transportation between the mainland and the islands.

Our first port of call was Port Au Prince, Haiti. Our picture was to be about voodoo and Port Au Prince was the voodoo capital of the world. Here, in the center of the voodoo religion, our company prop man expected to find many of the things with which to dress the sets so that they would look like authentic places of voodoo worship. It has always been true that a prop man — more correctly, a property master — can magically produce anything the director asks for, however unusual, even if he has to buy it, borrow it, beg it, or steal it. In the case of the props he needed for *Drums in the Night* — stuffed snake skins, goatskin drums, skulls, and other exotica — he couldn't buy them because they were sacred objects. Nor could he beg or borrow them, so there was nothing left but to steal them. Which he did.

George Terwilliger, the writer-director of the script, was an expert on voodoo, with several books on the subject to his credit. He was appalled when he learned how the props had been acquired. "Bad luck will follow," he said. "Very bad luck." Well, we'd see.

Kingston, Jamaica, was a lively city, full of calypso music, spicy odors, flying cockroaches as big as hummingbirds, loud talk, and louder laughter. It was like no place I had ever known.

The company was lodged at the Myrtle Bank Hotel in the heart of Kingston. The hotel's swimming pool was a rendezvous for a colony of young men who were called, I learned, "remittance men." Unwanted in their homeland for reasons of alcoholism, homosexuality, drugs, incorrigibility, or general misbehavior, they received sparse remittances from home on condition that they stay away. They were a charming group of scoundrels who supplemented their incomes by cadging from the hotel guests.

Richard Haydn was one of them, though the reasons for his inclusion were obscure. He didn't seem to share the amorality of the others. He had, in fact, a rich theatrical background in England. He attached himself to us.

On our first night in Kingston, Haydn offered to take us to a party. Hal Winthrop, our leading man, and I accepted.

The company had assigned a car and driver to us. The party was a short distance out of town on a ranch. As we approached we could hear the music and laughter half a mile away. The sounds carried well in the fragrant tropical night. The house was blazing with light. As we entered we were greeted by a young lady who, after introductions, took us to meet the host. He was an elderly man seated at the head of a table loaded with fruits and meats. He was dead.

He had died the night before. This was his farewell party. They were not about to put his body in the ground until, after a couple of days in the tropical climate, it had deteriorated to the point where it was of no use to anyone who might have wanted to convert it into a zombie.

It was a nice party, rather like an Irish wake. Before we left we said a polite goodbye to our host at the head of the table. He didn't respond.

Superstition was rampant in the islands. People did get sick under the influence of a voodoo curse, but the curse didn't work unless the victim learned that it had been put in effect. Since the curse was powerless unless the victim knew about it, it is clear that the power of suggestion was a potent factor — that the power of voodoo was due, at least in part, to the credulity and profound beliefs of its practitioners. The maid at the Myrtle Bank Hotel warned me to destroy my nail clippings and hair combings lest some evil person get hold of them and put them in a voodoo doll, thus gaining the power of life or death over me.

We started production, or, more accurately, attempted to start production. We set up for the first shots, which were to be night scenes in a forest grove. During the day the grips had set up the big arc lamps that were going to light the scene. They focused them on a huge cottonwood tree which was to be the background for the first setup. They brought in the cameras, sound equipment, generators, and everything that would be needed for the first scene when the command to "roll 'em!" would be given.

As twilight fell, the company was assembled to rehearse the scene we were about to shoot. As the evil overseer of the heroine's ranch, I was to be pursued by vengeful laborers. I was to make my stand in the gnarled crevices of a huge cottonwood tree. We rehearsed until the head cameraman judged that the darkness was complete enough for his purposes. He gave the command to start the generators and hit the sun arcs. In seconds the tree was flooded with light.

The assistant director shouted, "Ready to roll. Quiet on the set."

"Hold it!", the sound man called. "I get a buzzing sound. Check the carbons in the arc lights."

The buzzing wasn't in the arc lights. Now we all could hear it, growing louder, strangely threatening. Suddenly, painfully, we became aware of the source of the buzzing. Hornets! We were under attack! The little brutes had been startled awake when our lights hit the tree in which their hive was lodged, and they came out fighting. The angry hordes stuck their venomous stings into every exposed part of our bodies. We beat a panicky, scrambling retreat, leaving the field to the enraged winged warriors.

Nobody was untouched. Several required medical attention. Those who were allergic to the stings were hospitalized. By the time they recovered, we found ourselves three days behind schedule without having exposed a foot of film.

We got our first shots on what was to have been the fourth scheduled day. Towards the end of the first week we were to shoot a sequence at the beach. Our key grip, Dandy Andy, waded into the surf to set one of the huge reflectors. Waist deep in the water, suddenly he screamed. We watched as he scrambled toward shore and the water turned red around him. He staggered onto the beach streaming blood. Something, probably a giant barracuda, had torn a football-sized hunk of meat out of his thigh. He died from loss of blood before help arrived.

In the third week of production, Jack Cameron, our makeup man, died of yellow fever. I convinced our producer, Bill Saal, that there was no need to send for a replacement — Richard Haydn could pinch hit. He'd worked in the theatre, and besides he was British, which satisfied the quota requirements.

Dick Haydn saved the money he earned as makeup man for *Drums in the Night*, and bought himself a ticket to

New York on a banana boat. There, he auditioned for the Rudy Vallee radio show, got on the air doing fish imitations (Yeah! fish imitations!), was a big hit, got a picture contract, and wound up in Hollywood.

Another night sequence was scheduled early in the fol-1lowing week. It was to be cut into the chase as I was being pursued by the angry ranch hands. In the islands they frequently use a type of cactus which grows very tall and very dense as a sort of fence. The viciously-barbed plant is guaranteed to keep intruders out and livestock in. I was to run alongside a wall of the stuff, stumbling, falling, and rising to stagger on out of the shot.

To light the scene, two grips holding flares were to run along parallel to me, the flares throwing an eery, flickering light. It was a simple scene. We decided to do it without a rehearsal so as to save the flares.

We should have rehearsed.

The ground along the cactus fence was littered with fragments of the damned plant. Each time I fell — and I fell three times in the shot — I came up speared with the barbed quills as though I had wrestled with a porcupine.

Next stop, the hospital.

The barbed spines couldn't be plucked out. They had to be cut out. This was before antibiotics, so each cut became infected. We lost four more production days.

In the final week of shooting the assistant sound man fell off the sound boom and broke his neck.

We finished the picture five weeks behind what was to have been a six-week schedule. There'd been three deaths, countless misadventures, we were hundreds of thousands of dollars over budget, and I had lost eighteen pounds. Did it have anything to do with the things our prop man stole in Port Au Prince? Nah!

Back in New York, I found my professional status upgraded. Jed Harris was the Wonder Boy of the legitimate theatre in the thirties. The producer-director of *Coquette, The Royal Family, The Front Page*, and many other smash hits of the period, he called me in for an appointment.

I was agog with anticipation. A job in a Jed Harris production was an actor's dream. His plays ran forever. It turned out that it wasn't a play he wanted me for. It was something quite different. He wanted me as part of a goon squad he was organizing.

At the time, a rabble-rouser by the name of Joe McWilliams was preaching Hitler's doctrines to a receptive audience in Yorkville, the German section of Manhattan. Harris was enlisting as many Jewish hoodlums as he could gather together, to form a flying squad for the purpose of invading Yorkville with assault and battery in mind.

At a signal from Harris, the squad was to charge in and break up the McWilliams rallies with baseball bats and brass knuckles. Jed wanted me to be a part of this laudable enterprise. He would supply leadership, weapons, transportation, and bail money.

I declined. I explained that my wife had a thing about my getting arrested and, for that matter, so did I. So thanks, but no, thanks.

Although not many people had seen the short-lived *Hotel Alimony*, among those who had there was a considerable percentage of agents, producers, and directors — people who made a point of being up to date regarding casting possibilities. I got several offers and I had to make a decision, a dilemma that actors faced at the beginning of a season.

At that time there was a definite season. New production peaked in September, November, and December. Then the number of shows in production fell sharply, tapering off to a dead stop in the spring. Few legitimate theatres were air conditioned, and consequently the summer months were the theatrical doldrums. Few but the strong survived June, July, and August. An actor was likely to have most of his job opportunities in the fall and winter. If he passed up the play destined to be a hit and chose a flop because he got to wear character makeup, or because there were more sides to his part, he paid the penalty. Unless he picked up a meagerly-paying job in summer stock, it was back to his job behind the soda fountain in Whelan's Drug Store until next season.

I chose wisely, or at any rate, luckily. I wound up in a play called *Fly Away Home*, written by Dorothy Bennett and produced by Theron Bamberger. The cast included Thomas Mitchell, Montgomery Clift, Andrea King, and Albert Van Dekker, who dropped the "Van" when he went into pictures. The play was about the adventures and misadventures of a city family spending the summer on Cape Cod. I played a local Portuguese fisherman, complete with facial stubble and an accent.

My big scene was with Tommy Mitchell. Enraged by the rumor that Mitchell's fifteen-year-old son, played by fourteen-year-old Monty Clift, was fooling around with my adolescent daughter, I blustered on stage, threatening death and destruction. In the course of the scene, Mitchell soothed me and plied me with booze. Pretty soon we were pledging eternal friendship. It was a showcase scene for me. I got to play a wide range of emotions, from early rage to later boozy sentimentality. I loved it.

At an early stage in rehearsals Tommy took over the direction of the play from an incompetent director. He was dissatisfied with the way my scene was written. He promised to rewrite it and, until he got around to it, we were to skip the scene in rehearsals.

He never got around to it.

The rest of the play was rehearsed, polished, and perfected with a gaping ten-minute hole in the first act where my scene was supposed to be. I sat in the darkened theatre day after day watching my fellow actors gaining ease and confidence through rehearsal, while I waited for Tommy to get around to it.

Tommy was a noted ad libber. The story is told of how he coped with a problem during the run of *The Wisdom Tooth*. It seems that just as he and young Eddie Craven were about to make their entrance into a scene already in progress, a panicky stage manager rushed up to tell them that the third actor who was to play the scene with them was locked in the toilet with a jammed lock. The carpenter was working on the lock, and he'd get him out but it might take a few minutes and here comes your cue, for God's sake!

"Not to worry," said Tommy, the ad lib expert. Then to young Craven, "Come on. We'll just talk. Don't worry. I'll carry the whole thing. No problem."

They made their entrance. Taking Craven by the arm, he led him downstage center and said, "Okay, young man, tell me all about yourself."

Fly Away Home opened in Boston, at the Plymouth Theatre, for a two-week break in. On the way up on the train, with his back against the wall, Tommy called me in to his compartment. He said, "Okay, kid. You've been stalling long enough. Let's get to it. Here's how we'll do it. I'll say 'Hi, Gabriel. This is an unexpected pleasure,' and you'll say, 'What the hell's going on with that kid of yours,' and I'll say....."

And that's the way we did it when we opened the following night in Boston. The scene played like crazy. We got big laughs and I got a solid hand on my exit — and lovely notices.

The scene was never on paper. Later, Samuel French, which publishes plays for amateur presentation, bought the rights. Dismayed to find that this key scene wasn't in the script, they sent a stenographer who stood in the wings and took down our ad-libs in short hand.

It was a nice play; and it had a nice run. Young Monty Clift developed the habit of coming to the dressing room I shared with Van Dekker, while we were making up. He would sit quietly, listening to our salty anecdotes. A couple of months into the run, my wife and I got a totally unexpected invitation to dinner at the home of Monty's parents. Oh oh, I figured. Here it comes. "Young man, I wish you would moderate your language in my son's presence."

The Clift's apartment was elegant. Clift senior exuded prosperity, and the dinner was served by a butler and a maid. In the library, over after-dinner coffee, Mrs. Clift, an attractive, fortyish woman, highly-styled, with an aristocratic bearing, revealed the reason for our invitation. "I want to thank you," she said, "for exerting a healthy influence on Monty. He has been raised in a sheltered environment. Perhaps he has been over-protected. His adolescent contacts were carefully selected. When I allowed him to go into the theatre I feared that I was making a mistake, but, from what Monty tells me about the time he spends with you and Mr. Van Dekker, I gather that you have had a toughening effect on him. He needed that to prepare him for life. And he seems to have enjoyed the Rabelaisian environment you have created. I want to thank you."

Rabelaisian?

By the way, Monty's father scarcely opened his mouth through dinner.

Just as Monty visited Van Dekker and me, I had developed the habit of visiting Tommy's dressing room before the curtain went up. Frequently he came to the theatre somewhat illuminated. I would watch, in bemused amazement, as he heeded the call of "Curtain going up." He would stagger to the door though which he was to enter, finger his fly to make sure it was zipped, step across the threshold and become the consummate professional, skillful and self assured.

On one occasion, when I visited Tommy's dressing room he had a visitor, Tallulah Bankhead. I was awestruck. We were introduced, we shook hands, and then I heard that famous voice offering me a drink.

I said, "No, thanks. I never drink before I go on."

Can you believe it?

As soon as the words were out of my mouth I'd have given my new stainless-steel-shafted golf clubs to have them back. Instead I got the hell out of Tommy's dressing room.

Shortly thereafter, I got my cue and made my entrance on stage. As I was about to start my dialogue, my eyes caught a flicker of movement downstage left. There was Bankhead leaning over the sill of a downstage window, out of the audience's sight lines. She thumbed her nose, stuck out her tongue, and gave me a silent bird.

Up I went — into the stratosphere. I couldn't remember a line. Hell, I couldn't remember my name! Every time my eyeballs overcame my frantic efforts to keep them pointed stage right, there she was, downstage left, making horrible faces.

I must have gotten through the scene, but I don't know how.

Late in our run, George Abbott offered me a lead role in a road company of his smash hit, *Three Men on a Horse*, at a lot more money than I had ever gotten. He upped me to two hundred and fifty a week over the piteous protests of his producer, Alex Yokel, of whom more will be heard later.

Regretfully, I gave my two-weeks notice to the management of *Fly Away Home*. The time came when I made an entrance to play my scene with Tommy for the last time. Things proceeded normally till we reached the point where Tommy was to press on me the first of what was to be a series of drinks. Unsuspecting, I lifted the well-filled cup to my lips and an unexpected but familiar odor hit my nostrils. Hold it! This was not the traditional cold tea that we had sloshed down more than a hundred times in the course of this scene. This, goddam it, was whiskey!

What to do? Ad lib a line like "No thanks. I'm driving," and make an exit? No. There was a gleam in Tommy's eye. I'd fix him. If I drank the stuff, he'd have to drink it. He had to match me drink for drink, and I was not the downy-cheeked amateur he took me for! After all, I had trained during the prohibition days on bootleg whiskey and gin made in the fraternity house bathtub. Let's go!

Ten minutes later I staggered off stage and collapsed in my dressing room while Tommy continued his performance as though he had been drinking malted milk.

Three Men on a Horse was an enormously successful comedy about a clairvoyant greeting card writer with a talent for picking winning horses. In the road company, I played the part that Sam Levene had created in New York. A minor rivalry had been developing between Sam and me, since we tended to come up for the same parts. We were not unlike in appearance and, if the part required it, I could fall into the same stylized delivery that Sam used. Sam watched my developing career with an eagle eye. He was fiercely defensive of his territory.

The dress rehearsal for my company was held on a weekday afternoon, in the Playhouse Theatre, using the original company's sets and props. The house was filled with an invited audience. My wife, teaching biology in the New York high school system, didn't get to the theatre until shortly after the performance had started. To avoid disturbing the audience, she stood in the back of the darkened house.

Someone was pacing back and forth in the shadows behind her. It was Sam. He wasn't watching the stage, but he was listening. He was checking every laugh I got against what he was accustomed to. At one point, for whatever reason, I got an enormous laugh followed by applause.

Without missing a step, Sam snarled into my wife's ear, "What did he do? Drop his pants?"

The itinerary for the road company of *Three Men on a Horse* crisscrossed the country, from corner to corner — quite literally. We played the show from the Pacific Northwest to the Florida keys, and from New England to Southern California. We were scheduled for extended runs in the major cities, a week or two in the secondary cities, and split weeks and one-night stands in the boondocks.

Until the early thirties, the road had been an important contributor to the welfare of the legitimate theatre. Local stock or repertory companies proliferated throughout the country. They fed the Broadway stage with writing, acting, and directing talent. They were, so to speak, the minor league in which the players got ready for the majors. Of equal importance, the theatres they occupied provided stages for the touring companies that came through periodically.

When a show came to the end of its Broadway run, it could milk the road for a couple of extra years under the motto "Fresh from its Broadway run, with the original New York cast, for three nights only at Rubin's Chinese Theatre!"

If your show was a real smash in New York, you would probably organize one or more road companies to multiply your earnings, as in the case of *Three Men on a Horse*.

Unhappily, when we started on the road a change had taken place. In the late twenties, under the stunning impact of talking pictures, the theatres which had housed the local companies converted to movies as fast as they could get the equipment. Consequently, as soon as a stage company left the major cities, it ran out of real theatres. We played our split weeks and one night stands in skating rinks, high school auditoriums, tabernacles, boxing rings — anyplace where we could mount our sets and place seats.

My marriage was still quite new, and the separation was a hardship. When we played an extended engagement, and if, happily, it coincided with Frankie's vacations from teaching, she would join me in San Francisco, New Orleans, or wherever, bearing champagne and caviar with which to celebrate what amounted to an extra honeymoon.

The things I remember about the year on the road with *Three Men* are the visits from my wife, the hardships of a long stretch of one-nighters, when our Pullman car was our hotel and a shower was a great luxury, the infinite variety of our beautiful states, and the horrible incident in San Francisco when I pinned Percy Kilbride to the bed sheets.

Our production was set up on a revolving stage, a sort of turntable. While a given scene was playing in front of the audience, the following scene was in the wings, on the turntable, waiting to be swung into place. This setup eliminated the delays of scene changing, which was of particular importance with a fast-paced comedy such as ours. Delays between scenes can kill tempo.

In this case we were waiting in the wings in a set representing a shabby hotel bedroom, Eddie Craven playing Charlie, Frank Otto playing Harry, and me, Patsy, the leader of the trio. Percy Kilbride was Irwin, the psychic greeting card writer with a supernatural talent for picking winning racehorses. Irwin was in bed, clad in oversized long johns, recovering from a hangover. I sat on the bed, by his side, in the backstage darkness. As we waited to be swung into action I heard Percy mutter, "Darn!"

"What's the matter?"

"The pin. That darned diaper pin. It just popped open."

"Roll over on your side and I'll fix it."

Percy was thin and the winter woollies he wore were large. Consequently the flap in the back tended to gape. To prevent indecent exposure, Percy took up the slack with a large safety pin. I re-pinned him hastily as we were swung into place.

The footlights came up and we started the scene. On cue, when Percy crawled out of bed and staggered toward the bathroom, the bed sheet went with him! I had pinned him to the sheet!

Step by step he struggled on, trailing the bed sheet behind him like the train on the Queen's coronation gown. I attempted a rescue. As the sheet trailed by me, I stepped on it, hoping to give Percy a chance to tear loose. He didn't tear loose, but the flap in his underwear did!

That was it! Goodbye self-control, hello pandemonium!!!

It was a classic breakup such as I've never seen or heard of elsewhere. No use trying to repress our hysteria. No use trying to continue with the dialogue. Ring down the curtain!

Sometime later, when we had regained control and repaired Percy's trap door, the curtain was raised and we tried again. No use. When we got to Percy's cue to get out of bed, we broke up again. By now the audience was enjoying the situation more than the play. We got started on the third try, much to the audience's regret.

I'm sure that every ticket holder who was in the Geary Theatre on that historic occasion dined for weeks thereafter on the retelling of the saga of the time when Percy Kilbride's ass was out.

Shortly before Easter I gave my two-weeks notice to the company manager. Except for her occasional visits, I had been away from my wife for a whole year. I had made what was a lot of money for me, and I was tired of the show. The Easter-week layoff was pending; and I didn't relish the idea of spending an idle week in a Minneapolis hotel room.

At that time, because of the traditionally poor business in those periods, Actor's Equity permitted a company to shut down for the weeks preceding Christmas and Easter without paying salaries.

When my two weeks notice expired, I hopped a train for New York. So that we could spend some of my accumulated wealth, we were planning our first trip to Europe as soon as Frankie's school term ended.

Soon after my return to New York I ran into Albert Van Dekker on Broadway. He gave me a strange greeting. "You've gotten yourself into a hell of a mess! What is it with you? Did you go crazy?"

Van Dekker was a member of the Equity council which adjudicated complaints pertaining to actors. I learned that shortly after I had given my notice, Alex Yokel, the nominal producer of *Three Men*, had appeared before the council, petitioning for permission to rehearse the company without pay during the Easter layoff. Such permission was seldom granted. This case was special, Yokel claimed, because my flagrant misconduct had created an emergency. According to him, my chronic tardiness, frequent drunkenness, and general misbehavior had made it necessary to dismiss me and train a replacement. Hence the petition.

I excused myself from Van Dekker and made my way to the Strand Theatre building where Alex Yokel had his office. Yokel was known as "Twitchy Tit" because of a tic which had him constantly shrugging his coat into place.

I was going to kill him. I knew just how I was going to do it. I'd knock him down and pound his head against the pavement until he stopped moving.

Yokel occupied one of the offices in a complex rented by Warner Bros., the actual backers and owners of *Three Men*.

"Which is Yokel's office?" I demanded of the receptionist.

"Who shall I tell him..."

"Never mind," and I vaulted over the low railing.

I burst into several offices succeeding only in startling the occupants, none of whom were Yokel. Emerging from one office I heard the clatter of running feet in the corridor.

I turned and there was old Twitchy Tit making it for a rear exit. The receptionist had warned him.

I went after him.

Down the stairs and out onto Broadway. I couldn't gain on him though I was younger and better conditioned. I was driven by rage, but he was inspired by terror, which is a better motivator. Heading south, he made it safely across Forty-Sixth Street, while I was held up by the traffic. That enforced pause saved my future. In that brief moment my brain asserted control over my adrenal glands. "What are you doing, *schmuck*?" it demanded. "You're about to blow everything — your trip to Europe, your plans for a family, your career, your whole future!"

A half a block ahead of me on Broadway I saw the frantically wobbling ass of the departing fugitive.

"Yeah. Guess you're right," my adrenals said to my brain. I turned around, walked up Broadway, turned into the nearest bar, and ordered a double Jack Daniels.

Our European vacation was a smashing success. We sailed to Europe on board the Statendam, student class (a euphemism for third class, which, in turn, is a euphemism for steerage). We spent two weeks in London in a bed-and-breakfast lodging on Tavistock Square; ten days in Paris, where I bought three original Lautrec posters for seven dollars apiece; a week in Venice in a delightful, albeit flea-infested, pensione; a week in Rome in a pensione by the Roman Forum; a week in Capri at the Hotel Quisisana; and home second-class on the Conte De Savoia because we couldn't stand the open-pit toilets in third class. We were gone two months; and the total cost from door to door was eleven hundred and fifty dollars, so help me!

three

Light the Lights!

Refreshed and eager after our vacation, I tackled Broadway and I got lucky. Marc Connelly, author of *Green Pastures, Dulcy, Merton of the Movies*, and many other successful plays, was to direct a new production about romance in the Borscht Belt. I read for him and he liked me. *Having Wonderful Time*, written by Arthur Kober, was about a summer encounter in a Catskill Mountain resort cleverly named Kamp Kare Free. Teddy Stern, a guest, meets Chick Kessler, a waiter, and their romance blossoms until threatened by a lecherous millinery salesman with a penchant for "genuine Italian silk shirts." The luminous Katherine Locke played "Teddy," Julie (later John) Garfield played "Chick," and I played the lecherous heavy.

Because of the locale, Mr. Connelly drew heavily on the Yiddish theatre for his cast. He enlisted Wolfe Barzell, Shimen Ruskin and Hudy Bleich. They were a delightful, upbeat crew of bohemians. They became my friends; and during the run of the play they introduced me to the lore of the Second Avenue Theatre, the home of the Yiddish theatre in New York. *Having Wonderful Time* had a smash opening. We skipped the out-of-town break-in and opened cold on Broadway, because the producers felt that only New York audiences would understand and accept the Borscht Belt characters. When they made a musical out of *Having Wonderful Time*, they Aryanized it from top to bottom, even though all our reviews had stressed the fact that the unique color and idiom of the Catskill culture was our principal asset. They called it *Wish You Were Here*. Oh, well. I suppose they knew what they were doing, since the show had a run of almost six hundred performances.

I enjoyed the indescribable excitement of a successful Broadway opening for the second time. In later years, in Hollywood, that was the thing about legit that I missed most. I didn't miss the equally indescribable depression of a flop.

We were off to a long, happy run. Garfield and I shared a dressing room. A warm relationship resulted. Julie was an "Angelo Patri boy." Angelo Patri ran a school for disadvantaged and problem children. Julie had been both. Patri had straightened him out, and after some troubled years, Julie had wound up with the Group Theatre.

The Group paid its members very little money. When Julie got the chance to work in the commercial theatre — which is how the Group referred to non-Group theatrical activity — he requested and was granted permission to take a leave, providing he kept himself ready to return to the Group when called. He was scheduled for the lead in a play that Odets was writing. It was to be called *Golden Boy*.

When he landed the lead in *Wonderful Time*, he was flat broke. He owed three months back rent on a cold water flat on Twenty-Third Street, and his wife, Robbie, was wearing a discarded man's suit jacket in lieu of a winter overcoat. The three hundred dollars a week that he was paid during the run of the show was a lifesaver. By the third week of our run, Robbie was wearing a regular overcoat.

Julie and I enlisted together in Benno Schneider's acting class. It was held once week in a loft over a theatre on lower Fifth Avenue. All the students were in the professional theatre, taking the class to stretch their acting muscles. The roster included several who were to go on to distinguished careers — among them Burgess Meredith, Kitty Carlisle, and Arlene Frances. Students were required to prepare an exercise for each weekly session, a scene from a play or a characterization, to be viewed and criticized by Benno and the members of the class. On one occasion Julie and I chose a scene from *Othello*. He was to be Iago and I was to be the Moor.

We rehearsed the scene in our dressing room and performed it for the class at the designated time. I thought we did a pretty good job, and apparently the class thought so too. Their comments were mildly favorable. Then Benno took over. He gave Julie faint praise, but much reassurance.

"You did well, considering your lack of experience with the Shakespearean idiom," he said. "You tried to show what Iago thought as well as what he did, and that was good...." and so on. Then he turned to me. "How dare you!" he thundered. "How can you attempt one of the greatest roles in the theatre with so little understanding? What do you know about Othello? How old is he? Where was he born? How much education does he have?"....and on and on. By the time he was through with me I was a basket case. Years later, in Hollywood, where he was coaching at a studio, I recalled the incident to him.

"I never understood why you were so gentle with Garfield and so brutal with me," I told him. "We were both equally lousy."

"It was my habit to cut the cloth to fit the customer," he told me. "Julie needed reassurance and you needed humility."

I was sorry I'd asked.

Late in the season Julie learned that the lead role in The Group's planned production of *Golden Boy* was not to go to him. The internal politics of The Group, a very political organization indeed, had led to the decision that the role, a star maker, was to be awarded to Luther Adler, who had more seniority in the Group than Julie. Julie was designated to play the role of a cab driver. Naturally, he was desolate.

Just at that time he got a bid from Hollywood. Warner Bros. offered him a job in a picture with a four-week guarantee at seven-fifty a week. Although I was only six years older than he, Julie had come to consider me as a sort of Dutch uncle. He asked for my advice.

I told him, "Let's be realistic. You must not go back to The Group to play a minor role after playing a lead on Broadway. That's a career step backward. As for Hollywood, so they'll pay you seven hundred and fifty for four weeks, but *Having Wonderful Time* is going to run forever, and in the long run you'll make a lot more staying here. It's not as though making a picture would open up a new career for you. It's a one-shot. Let's face it. You're not the Hollywood leading man type. Stay where you are, Julie. You'd never make it in Hollywood."

That advice is often quoted as an example of my talent for the early recognition of star quality.

As a matter of fact, I wasn't that far wrong. Nobody knew it, but audiences were ripe for the anti-hero. In his first picture, *Four Daughters,* Julie brought to the screen a new kind of leading man, rugged, cynical, world-weary, but vulnerable. His was an unprecedented success.

Marc Connelly, the director of *Having Wonderful Time,* made me his protégé. He involved me in his weekly twenty-five-cent-limit poker games. He took me to lunch at the Algonquin Round Table, of which he was a charter member, and he set me to work reading unsolicited play scripts. I was paid five dollars per script for reading, summarizing, and making a recommendation.

Producers got unsolicited scripts by the dozen. The middle range of producers, that is to say those below the Olympian level of the Shuberts and The Theatre Guild, seldom got a crack at the good stuff. That came by way of reputable agents and went directly to one of the majors. They got the pick of the crop before it ever reached the market. Eugene O'Neill's output went directly to The Theatre Guild. Guthrie McClintic got first shot at a Maxwell Anderson script. Clare Booth's output was likely to go to Brock Pemberton. The less well-established producers were reduced to combing through unsolicited manuscripts in the hope of finding another *Three Men on a Horse.*

It was an indisputable fact that ninety percent of the successful plays came from ten percent of the authors. Fringe producers had to dig deep to find the script with which to make the open ten percent, and that's why I was getting five dollars a script. To find a sleeper. It was hard work and the pay was pitiful, but the long range benefits were great. Reading, analyzing, and dissecting countless scripts was precious training for what was to become my career. When I read that Michelangelo learned anatomy by dissecting cadavers, I thought, "Me, too."

Marc Connelly gave me a chance to direct a road company of *Having Wonderful Time*, but it was not a road company in the sense of *Three Men on a Horse*, with an itinerary that spanned the nation. Because of its ethnic nature, it was judged that it would have limited appeal outside of the New York area, so our road company went out on what was called the Subway Circuit. A couple of nickel-and-dime producers, Wee and Leventhal, had put together a circuit of theatres that included Brighton Beach, Brooklyn, the Bronx, Newark, and Providence.

Meanwhile, the original company was still rolling along.

An odd-looking person came to audition for a job in the road company. His name was Solen Bury. He came into my office, one of a train of actors who had shown up when the word got around that I was casting. He didn't look at all like what I wanted for the open bit parts. I was looking for fresh-faced college-boy types to play waiters in a Catskill Mountain adult camp. Sol was bushy-haired, sallow, and thirtyish. I exchanged a few routine words with him, asked a few standard questions, and was set to brush him off with the "Don't call us, we'll call you" formula. However, he anticipated me.

"Don't give me no bullshit," he told me. "You ain't gonna put me in your show, because I ain't pretty like them fags out there. You're like all the rest of them. You don't know if I got talent and you don't give a damn."

All of a sudden I found myself backing off. I was practically apologizing to this rude son of a bitch! "You've got me all wrong. You've got just as good a chance as any of those kids out there. You don't have to be pretty. As a matter of fact, you look interesting. Different."

Before I knew it, I had talked myself into hiring the guy.

Some months later, Sol told me how he had developed his shock technique for use in interviews.

"When I was like fourteen years old," he told me, "I had pimples. Boy, did I have pimples! I had pimples on my pimples! I used to go to the dances wid the fellers but no girl would ever dance wid me. How could you blame 'em? I was a mess. The other guys was all dancin', but I used to just sit while they was havin' fun. One time I got mad. I says to myself, 'the hell wid it!' and I goes up to dis nice-lookin' chick and I says, 'I suppose you ain't gonna dance wid me because I got pimples. Maybe I'm the best dancer in the whole joint, but you don't care, because I got pimples! Right?' And she kinda stammers, and her face gets red, and she says, 'Well, that don't bother me. I mean, well, I don't really mind....' So I says 'Okay. Let's dance' and dat's what we do. So since then I figger you gotta hit 'em before they have a chance to put their guard up and dat's what I do."

Ultimately we became friends. He introduced me to burlesque, that cradle of pragmatic showmanship, but our acquaintanceship would not have survived that first meeting if it were not for his unique approach to job hunting.

In November of 1937, I got a red hot offer to play the lead in *Siege*, written by Irwin Shaw, author of *Bury the Dead*. It was to be produced by Norman Bel Geddes, producer of *Street Scene*, and directed by Chester Erskine, director of *The Last Mile*, *Subway Express*, and many others. Those were very distinguished auspices.

I was to play a romantic lead with a big boost in salary, and the deal allowed me stay with *Wonderful Time* until just before *Siege* opened.

It was a spectacular production. Bel Geddes, at that time the leading designer for the stage, had gone all out. He had created a massive set to represent the Alcazar in Toledo during the Spanish Rebellion. It was a huge creation, towering over the stage like Mount Everest. It could turn three hundred and sixty degrees. It could light up interior sets behind a scrim. It could shudder under the impact of cannon fire. It could do everything but recite the dialogue. It was enormously impressive. Trouble was, it diminished the actors who crept in it and around it — they were ants on an anthill. The critics destroyed us.

We had opened on December 8th. On December 10th a notice appeared in the personal columns of *The New York Times*. It read, "Sheldon, come home. All is forgiven. Cast and crew of *Having Wonderful Time*." *Siege* closed after six performances. The day after it closed I was back in the cast of *Wonderful Time*, having missed only eight performances.

Wonderful Time closed early in 1938 and I was picked up almost immediately by Antoinette Perry — the "Tony" after whom the "Tony" awards are named — for the play she was about to direct. *Kiss the Boys Goodbye* was written by Clare Booth. It satirized the hullabaloo that accompanied the search for an actress to play Scarlett O'Hara in David O. Selznick's upcoming production of *Gone With The Wind*. The character I played was a thinly-disguised version of Selznick. In the second act, clad in pajamas and a robe, I knocked on the bedroom door of the latest candidate for the role of Scarlett O'Hara. When she refused to let me in I said, in shocked surprise, "But, dear, I'm a producer!" Somehow I was becoming a specialist in on-stage lechery.

Kiss the Boys Goodbye was a major hit. Boy, was I on a roll! It was never made into a picture because the movie industry was not partial to self-satirization.

The year-and-a-half run of *Kiss* was uneventful except for two things. The first was the extraordinary Christmas present that Clare Booth gave the cast. She took over New York's leading night club, El Morocco, for New Year's Eve. She gave each of us a table for sixteen, for dinner, supper, and breakfast, with unlimited champagne with which to float the New Year in. Did we build up Brownie points with our guests!

The second memorable occurrence, late in the run, was a call from Hollywood. I was to report to MGM to work in a *Thin Man* picture with Myrna Loy and William Powell.

The year was 1939. Actually, I had committed to the picture almost a year earlier, but it had been postponed when Powell was stricken with cancer of the colon. The dramatic surgery that was necessary to cope with that type of cancer was relatively new and still comparatively crude. Powell had come through it well and was ready to go to work, but the suave, urbane, glamorous star had to cope with the indignity of a colostomy bag.

I had to do a fight scene with him. "Be gentle with him," I was warned.

Someone should have told him to be gentle with me. When we shot the scene the recuperating invalid tossed me around like a beach ball.

He was a remarkable man. Some years ago I visited with him in Palm Springs. He was well into his eighties, looking tan and fit, and still playing an excellent game of tennis.

Hollywood. A widely misused term. The real Hollywood is an area bounded, roughly, on the east by Vermont Avenue and on the West by La Brea Avenue. In common usage, however, the term is used to include everything from Culver City to the San Fernando Valley.

I arrived in Hollywood via a trimotor plane. The trip took sixteen hours and the plane made five stops. The sleeping accommodations on board were regular, full-length, Pullman-type berths. However, since the planes weren't pressurized, you had to be careful to sleep on your stomach or your back. If you slept on your side with your ear pressed against the pillow, chances were that you'd wake up with a fearful earache because the down ear would have difficulty adjusting to the frequent changes of pressure that resulted from the takeoffs and landings.

Shortly after noon, we landed in L.A. I was met at the airport by a representative of the Leland Hayward Agency, who hustled me off to the Beverly Wilshire Hotel, where a room had been reserved for me. He gave me just enough time to check in, splash cold water on my face, change to a fresh shirt, before hustling me off to the studio where *Another Thin Man* was being shot. The production had started a few days earlier, and the director, W. S. [Woody] VanDyke, was waiting to see what the New York casting office had stuck him with.

Major Woodward S. VanDyke II, U.S.M.C., retired, was lounging in his canvas-backed director's chair, sipping a cup of coffee-colored liquid, which, by its odor, was largely gin. We were introduced. He looked me up and down. Apparently I was acceptable, because he nodded to my agent. The business part of our meeting was over, the social part was about to begin.

"Just got in, kid?" he asked.

"A couple of hours ago, Mr. VanDyke."

"The name is Woody. Where are you staying?"

"I'm checked in at the Beverly Wilshire."

He held up his nearly-empty cup for a refill. "Bozzy" Boswell, his first assistant, hurried over to pour from a coffee pot conspicuously labeled, "Director only. DO NOT TOUCH!"

VanDyke turned to my agent. "That's where you put him? The kid's going to be here two, maybe three months. You don't want him stuck in a hotel all that time."

"Two or three months?" I asked.

"At least."

"My guarantee is only for four weeks."

"Yeah, I know. Maybe we'll finish principal photography in four weeks but then there's the retakes and the added scenes."

In the course of time, I learned that VanDyke's approach to a shooting schedule was unique. He made no secret of it. In his words, "I finish the picture nice and fast. No fooling around. Print take one. I finish three or four days ahead of schedule and they give me a bonus. Then I go back and really make my picture."

It was not uncommon for VanDyke to take longer on his retakes than on his original production.

"A hotel isn't right for you, kid," he told me. He called Bozzy over.

"Let's knock it off, Bozzy."

"It's only four o'clock!"

"Yeah, I know. Gotta find the kid a place to live."

He dismissed my agent and took me in his car. His idea of orienting me was to display his own life style. He had four domiciles scattered from Hollywood to Malibu. The first one that we visited was in the Chateau Marmont, just off Sunset and La Cienega.

Two bedrooms, a living room, den and kitchen, all neatly furnished, undoubtedly by a studio set decorator, with furniture from the studio storerooms. The apartment also featured a fully supplied wet bar in the den.

The second pad was in the Wilshire Palms, on Wilshire Boulevard in Beverly Hills. There, the decorator's scheme featured zebra stripes, and the bar was built into the bookshelves.

The third domicile was in Malibu. The decorative scheme was nautical, and the bar opened out onto a sun deck.

We wound up that evening in the fourth and principal residence, in Brentwood. It was spacious, sumptuous, and in excellent taste. A houseboy served dinner. I think VanDyke was a widower — at any rate, there was no Mrs. VanDyke. After dinner we retired to the bar.

Bear in mind that this was the summer of 1939. Woody's bar featured a huge world globe, more than three feet in diameter. As the hour grew later, he showed me, by way of the globe, why the worsening European situation had to lead to war. Hitler was committed to expansion. Look at the map. Where can he expand? Here, into Poland. That will bring in England and France. Then he's got to move into Russia. Forget about his treaty with Stalin. You think that's going to hold him back?

Major W.S. VanDyke, U.S.M.C., retired, must have been a very good marine.

Time ticked away. I was moderately polluted and thoroughly fascinated, but as the eastern sky reddened I remembered that I had my first day in front of Hollywood cameras ahead of me and I had to break away. My call was for six-thirty a.m. in makeup.

Woody wakened his houseboy to drive me back to my hotel. I ordered a pot of coffee from room service, stood under the shower for half an hour, dressed, called a cab, and shortly thereafter reported to Stage Nineteen on the Metro-Goldwyn-Mayer lot for my first day on *Another Thin Man*.

Fresh as a daisy, Woody was again lounging in his canvas backed chair, sipping a cup of pseudo coffee. He greeted me.

"You look terrible, kid. You've got big circles under your eyes. If you hope to make it in this business you gotta take better care of yourself."

Woody VanDyke taught me a lot.

Early in the shooting schedule there was a scene in which I was to be shot while trying to scale a parapet. When the bullet hit me, I was to stagger, then fall onto the narrow top of the parapet, balance there briefly, then tumble off onto a pile of mattresses off-camera. It was tricky. The damned parapet was narrow and the surface was covered with gravel. Every time I hit it I left skin behind, not to mention the cuts and bruises that I carried away with me. Take after take, either I flinched, thus lousing up the shot, or VanDyke wasn't pleased with it for some other reason. When he finally okayed a print, I was a mess of scrapes and bruises. He called me over.

He said, "Look, kid. I just gave you a first class screwing. I took advantage of your inexperience. Don't ever let any other director make you do stuff like that. Don't even sit down in a hard chair without calling for a stunt man. That's how they make their living. When you do hazardous stuff you're keeping a qualified stunt man from making a paycheck. They're a tight group and they don't like things like that. One day you'll be doing a fight scene somewhere without a stuntman and a fist will come flying out of nowhere and you'll be picking your teeth up off the floor."

Yes, I learned a lot from W.S.VanDyke.

On a Thursday, late in the schedule, when we wrapped for the day, Bozzy gave me the welcome news that I was not on call Friday. At the time I was a house guest with the Brombergs. My old mentor, Joe, was comfortably relocated in Beverly Hills with a thriving movie career. Joe and

Goldie, his wife, were planning a weekend in Tijuana across the border from San Diego. It was an easy three-hour drive from Los Angeles. Tijuana had become the movie colony's playground with open gambling, bullfights, a race track, duty free shopping, and very good beer. I could join them for an extended weekend if Bozzy let me off the hook.

"Am I on standby?" I asked him.

When you were on standby you were expected to be reachable by phone in case there was a change in the schedule.

Bozzy said, "No. You're clear. We've got a full day's work with Powell and Loy."

Off I went to old Mexico with Joe and Goldie. The previous night she had had a memorable experience with their children, Marcia and Conrad. Joe prompted her to tell me about it.

Quite recently, Goldie had given birth to the Bromberg's third child. Just last night she had been confronted by Marcia, age eight, and Conrad, six. They demanded a showdown. They wanted to know exactly how mother had gotten that lump in her stomach which had turned out to be their sibling.

Goldie drew a breath. This was it. The dreaded confrontation that every parent had to face in those unsophisticated days before the modern school system took the burden of sex education off the parents' shoulders. The children listened with profound attention while Goldie used every narrative tool at her command — metaphor, analogy, hyperbole, and poetry — to explain how the father plants the seed in his beloved. Not only how, but where and with what.

The job well done, Goldie treated herself to a moment of self-congratulation. The children exchanged glances, then eight-year-old Marcia spoke.

"But, mother," she said. "That's fucking."

We had a lovely three-day weekend in Tijuana. I won thirty dollars at the races, cheered a brave toreador, booed a cowardly one, and had my fill of good Mexican beer. We got back to Beverly Hills to find the Bromberg household in a state of panic. The studio had been trying to reach me all day Friday.

Nobody knew how to find us. They had done everything but call out the police. Bill Powell had had a setback and couldn't work. They were forced to reshuffle the schedule. When they couldn't reach me they had to shut down for the day. It was a disaster. Tens of thousands of dollars up the chimney!

Monday morning I reported to the studio prepared to clear myself. It wasn't my fault. I wasn't on standby. Bozzy had cleared me. I started to explain this to VanDyke but he cut me short.

"I know about it," he said. "Bozzy told me. In a case like this they'll probably fine you a day's pay, but if you explain to them how Bozzy cleared you, you'll save a couple of hundred bucks and Bozzy will be out on the street. Out of a job. Decide what you want to do."

"I'm sorry I misunderstood Bozzy," I told him. "I'm new out here and I didn't understand what he meant when he told me, very clearly, that I was on standby."

It turned out to be an excellent investment. Woody moved my remaining scenes to the end of the shooting schedule, thereby gaining me two extra weeks' pay. Since I had been able to command a thousand-dollar-a-week salary, I returned to New York with a well-lined purse.

In New York Clare Booth was waiting for me with an offer to play the lead in a road company of her hit show, *Margin For Error*. In the original company the part had been created by Sam Levene. Here I was, treading in his footsteps once again. I was to play Police Officer Finkelstein, assigned to guard the home and person of the Nazi Consul.

The company was directed by Otto Preminger, the most feared director in the theatre. I found him to be a talented director and a pleasant companion. He wasn't at all the beast he was reputed to be. He was merely a Prussian, accustomed to making every suggestion sound like a command and every criticism like a death sentence.

We were on the road for four months, during which there was the time I caught Tallulah Bankhead with her pants down, and the time a whole audience disappeared.

The Bankhead incident occurred in Boston, the first stop in our road tour. We were playing the Plymouth Theatre. Our stage door was right across an alley from the stage door of the theatre where Bankhead was appearing in *The Little Foxes*.

One night, after the performance, Preminger suggested to me that we drop in on his old friend, Bankhead. I agreed eagerly, anxious to erase the impression my doltish behavior must have left five years earlier.

We crossed the alley where the stage doorkeeper directed us to the star's dressing room. Preminger knocked and that famous voice bade "Come in." We entered. Bankhead was not in her dressing room. She was in the adjacent john, the door of which was wide open, insouciantly sitting in plain view on the toilet.

"Make yourselves comfortable, darlings. I'll only be a minute."

She finished her business, flushed the toilet, and swept into the dressing room like the great lady she was.

The incident of the disappearing audience took place in Palm Beach where we were booked for a one-week engagement. Our opening there was a uniquely glamorous experience. Palm Beach was, and still is, the center of a tremendous concentration of wealth. The homes were enormous, and the women who lived in them were the epitome of bejeweled high style.

On the night of our opening, a parade of limousines discharged their glamorous cargoes at the entrance to our theatre. The first act of our play was enthusiastically received by the glittering audience that filled the auditorium from side to side. When the curtain rose for the second act the theatre was half empty. The beautiful people were gone.

"What happened?" I asked the house manager.

"It's always that way," he told me. "They come for the opening. The women see what all the other women are wearing and that's it. Off they go, back home."

Sam Lyons, the New York half of the agenting firm of Lyons and Lyons, had told me that when Paramount, which had bought *Having Wonderful Time*, was ready to put it into production, his brother, Arthur, the West Coast half of the firm, had been sure that he could set me to play the part I had originated in New York, providing that I came to the coast so they could do some tests.

Howver, Paramount 'goyed' the play up real good. Douglas Fairbanks, Jr. played Garfield's part. Ginger Rogers went in for Katherine Locke. Red Skelton, making his feature film debut, played the part of Itchy Flexner, camp social director, or tummeler, and Lee Bowman had been set for the part of Pinky Aaronsohn, the character I had played.

I went to the Lyons office in a high dudgeon. Sam heard me out and said he was sorry, but that Arthur could surely have gotten me the part if I had been in Hollywood and not three thousand miles away.

Now, the theatre was changing, and not for the better. Many of the stars who had lighted up the stage — Tallulah Bankhead, George M. Cohan, John Barrymore, Katherine Cornell, Ethel Barrymore — were at or near the end of their careers. The shoes they were leaving behind them would be hard to fill. The brilliant, vain, witty, eccentric, egotistic, generous, arrogant, selfish personalities, for whom the word "charisma" was coined, were departing, leaving legends in their wake.

Rising costs were smothering production in the theatre. In the twenties backers had been plentiful then. After all, investing on Broadway wasn't a potentially bank-breaking gamble. You could raise the curtain on a one-set show with a modest cast, for seven or eight thousand dollars. By the middle thirties the same show would cost fifteen or twenty thousand. We were heading into deep water, for by the end of the thirties costs had risen another fifty percent. And after that the whole thing got out of control. A runaway speedboat.

Inevitably, the volume of production fell off from year to year. In the middle twenties Broadway production reached a peak of eighty-six openings in a year. In 1931 there were still a gratifying eighty-two, but by 1939 the number had dropped to thirty-eight.

Rising costs and tight money weren't the only causes of the spectacular decline. In addition, there were rising prices at the box office, a talent drain, and talent defection.

Until the late thirties you could look to writers like Robert Sherwood, Elmer Rice, George Kaufman, Moss Hart, Maxwell Anderson, Eugene O'Neill, or their many contemporaries to feed the theatre's appetite for plays. In the ensuing years, for a variety of reasons, they stopped contributing.

Now that Hollywood was talking, the studios were seizing Broadway talent as fast as they could write the contracts. Few actors, writers, or directors could resist the siren call of big money — the "shining perversions" of films. The legitimate theatre no longer provided a career for most. For years, established talent had the reasonable expectation that their earnings in the theatre would be enough to support their life style. With production more than halved and declining further every year, that was no longer true.

It was customary for those of us in legit to look down upon the defectors to Hollywood. They were selling out, we said to one another. They were traitors, for whom money was more important than art. They were exchanging the challenge and inspiration of a live audience for the mechanical stare of a camera. Instead of the shining language of Shakespeare, they would be mouthing the uninspired words of anonymous hacks.

These noble sentiments would have been more meaningful if the people who expressed them were not so quick to rush home and pack a bag as soon as Hollywood beckoned.

Frankie and I were faced with a prime dilemma. From the first days of our marriage, she had earned eighteen hundred dollars a year as a biology teacher, and that bought a lot of groceries. The rent for our apartment in the stylish Central Park West area was sixty-five dollars a month. For the past few years, the theatre had been treating me well, with one job following the other. As a result, I had worked my salary up to an astronomical three hundred-fifty a week. With Frankie's regular income, we had been getting along nicely. If I went to California and scored well, my career would thenceforth center on films. Moving to the coast meant giving up what security we had for the unknown reefs of the movie business.

However, there were reasons, other than material ones, why leaving the theatre for Hollywood was traumatic. I was leaving behind a venue rich in tradition and colorful characters. We had just signed the lease for our comfortable apartment. We had furnished it with loving care. We had an eighteen-month-old baby daughter, Andy. Frankie had just received her coveted appointment as a permanent teacher, with tenure, in the New York City high school system. What we had represented security and comfort. What beckoned was a career change for me and a major sacrifice for my wife. The decision was in her hands.

The issue was never in doubt. Ever since the day when, as teenagers, we met and became high school sweethearts, Frankie had never put her interests ahead of mine. She took a leave from the New York City school system. I settled the lease on our apartment, bought a second-hand Ford two-door sedan for four hundred seventy-five dollars, filled a half-dozen nursing bottles with the baby's formula, packed Elsie (our German refugee maid) and the baby into the car, and — with seven hundred dollars in the bank — we were on our way.

California, here we come!

four

Camera Rolling!

The motion picture industry had been dominated by a handful of moguls in the pre-TV days. MGM was synonymous with L. B. Mayer. Paramount had Adolph Zukor. Twentieth Century-Fox had Darryl Zanuck. Harry Cohn was at Columbia. The Warner brothers had their own empire. So did Herb Yates at Republic. Carl Laemmle, "Uncle Carl," was at Universal. There were a couple of lusty independents like David O. Selznick and Sam Goldwyn, and that was it. Since there was no foreign competition, they had the field all to themselves.

It was easy to make fun of the moguls. For the most part, they were uneducated, and frequently vulgar and uncouth. Still, you couldn't change the fact that they had made pictures like *The Grapes of Wrath*, *The Wizard of Oz*, *Citizen Kane*, *Casablanca*, *Gone With the Wind*, *Stagecoach*, and the great catalogue of films that we now recognize as classics. They were the ultimate pragmatists, and they had a great yardstick for measuring what worked and what didn't: how much did it take in at the box office? If they liked the answer, they did it again.

The studios had big inventories of picture-making equipment. They owned vast real estate acreage. They had scores of writers, directors, and actors under contract, as well as set designers, cameramen, costume designers, and so on. They had sales and promotion organizations, distribution companies, and even theatres. They were totally self-sufficient.

The picture makers didn't kid themselves. Picture-making was an industry, not an art form, an entertainment form worlds apart from that which I left.

We arrived in Los Angeles in August of 1940. It had been a lovely drive except for one hideous stretch, crossing the desert in a car without air conditioning. On the plus side, there had been the Grand Canyon, the Rockies, the great plains, and the infinite variety of our cities and towns. Ours is, indeed, a noble country.

It took us a few days to get settled in. We found a nice little house in West Los Angeles, looked up a diaper service, and located the supermarkets. Finally, five days after our arrival, I was ready to meet with Arthur Lyons. I was anxious to do those tests and get my career started. I put on my freshly-laundered shirt with the Barrymore collar, Frankie selected an appropriate necktie, I donned my cleaned-and-pressed, dark grey suit, and off I went.

Arthur Lyons had offices on the ninth floor of the California Bank Building on Wilshire Boulevard. I had called ahead, so when I identified myself to the receptionist she waved me in to Mr. Lyons' office. He was a short, chubby, mustachioed man seated behind a vast desk and he greeted me thus, "Sheldon Leonard?"

"Yes, Mr. Lyons."

"I thought you were a short, blond feller."

Mr. Lyons soothed me with the assurance that everything would be all right. He would find something else for me. Something nice. Trust him.

I trusted him for three weeks, during which time I occupied myself by hitting golf balls on a nearby driving range, and catching calico bass off the half-day fishing boat from the Santa Monica pier. At the end of the third week, I put on the dark grey suit, and the shirt with the Barrymore collar, but no necktie, because nobody wore neckties in Southern California. I went to see Mr. Lyons.

"Mr. Lyons," I told him, "I've got to work. I've got a family to support. I need a job."

The little man got up from behind his vast desk, went to the window of his ninth floor office, and threw it open. He leaned out and shouted, "Hey, anybody! Sheldon Leonard needs a job."

A pause, then once again, louder, "Sheldon Leonard. A job. He needs a job."

A short pause, then he turned back into the room and said, "You heard somebody answer?"

A week later I found an agent who didn't think I was a short blond feller. Nat Goldstone got me a job in a picture at Twentieth Century-Fox at the same fee I had gotten for *Another Thin Man* — a thousand a week. *Tall, Dark and Handsome* was a modestly budgeted picture starring Cesar [Butch] Romero and Virginia Gilmore. The picture turned out surprisingly well. It was booked into the Radio City Music Hall, where it did good business, and was held over for four weeks.

Twentieth Century-Fox put me under a term contract, six hundred fifty dollars a week for forty weeks out of fifty-two, with options for renewals with salary increases over a seven-year period. Twenty-six thousand per annum, with twenty-six hundred off for agent's commission, was very nice money indeed in 1940. My bank account fattened up fast on that rich diet.

That was the good news. The bad news was that I had no control over the parts I played. That's the way it was. Either you did as you were told or you were put on suspension, and while you were on suspension you couldn't work any place else. The studio had placed me under contract because they liked the character I had played in *Tall, Dark and Handsome*, a suave, impeccably tailored, ruthless mob chief, and they were short on hoodlums. Warner Bros. had Cagney, Robinson, Bogart, Allen Jenkins, Frank McHugh and a host of lesser hoodlums, but Twentieth Century-Fox had none. For the term of my contract, I was expected to be suave but menacing for twenty-three thousand four hundred net per annum. But the government threw us a curve.

The war had created a shortage of film negative stock. What negative there was had been preempted by the army for the needs of the Signal Corps. The Office of War Information, however, acted on the premise that film was a major propaganda instrument, crucial in shaping the world-wide image of America and Americans. As a war measure, the OWI allocated film to the studios while warning them not to show an unflattering picture of our life style. Suave, menacing Sheldon Leonard and his ilk became *persona non grata.*

That blew it. Twentieth Century-Fox's plans to groom me to take my place alongside the Warner Bros. array of *goniffs* was out. I spent the rest of my stay at TC-F playing innocuous roles in films designed to exploit Betty Grable's wiggle or Carmen Miranda's bananas.

At the end of the second year, not surprisingly, the studio let my option lapse, but I was determined to make a place for myself in the film industry. Parenthetically, I dislike the use of the term "industry" when applied to a trade that is, or should be, creative. At any rate, I had become accustomed to Southern California living and I liked it. It was quite different from the live-by-night, sleep-by-day New York life style. In fact, by the beginning of the decade of the forties, the film community had created an environment that was different from that to be found anywhere else. Its population contained a high percentage of young, beautiful, extravagant, pampered people who couldn't be expected to behave like ordinary humans. Eccentricities were so common that it was almost eccentric not to have some.

One screen starlet, whose name has long since faded into obscurity, had four miniature French poodles, each dyed a different color to match her various ensembles.

A western star had an automobile custom-built with pistols for door handles, bull horns for radiator ornaments, and strawberry-roan-horsehide upholstery.

Although the colony was spread from Malibu to Newport, the heaviest concentration was in Beverly Hills. In north Beverly Hills to be precise, in the couple of square miles bounded on the east and west by Wilshire Boulevard and Doheny Drive and on the north and south by Sunset Boulevard and Santa Monica Boulevard. The streets in that area were heavily patrolled by the very efficient Beverly Hills police. Any pedestrian, day or night, was likely to be stopped and asked for identification. Rolls Royces were everywhere. Beverly Hills High School was in a class by itself. With sixteen working oil wells on its premises it could afford freshly-laundered pink workout suits every day for the gym classes, fluff-dried, pink towels pool side, and a track and football stadium of its very own. It was said that you could tell the faculty parking lot from the students' because it was the one with the old cars.

Dress throughout the community was super casual. Chasen's restaurant, run by the old vaudevillian Dave Chasen, was one of the few places in town where you could expect to find some male diners wearing neckties.

My wife had more trouble adjusting to the relaxed dress code than I did. To this day, her New York upbringing determines her dress style. She doesn't even own a pair of denims.

Studio commissaries were unique places. They were very democratic. Mega stars shared tables with secretaries. There was usually an executives' table, and probably one for writers or directors, but the mix throughout the room was thoroughly eclectic.

My agent was pleased with the fact that my contract wasn't renewed. He foresaw a period of greater variety in the parts I played, and he was right. Over the next eight years, I worked in fifty-seven pictures, playing everything from Mexican jailers to psychotic killers. Several things relating to those fifty-seven pictures come to mind.

Errol Flynn was a pain in the ass.

I had a couple of scenes with him in some obscure picture. As an actor, when I rehearsed a scene, I liked to find some business that would keep my hands occupied. Depending on what was available in the set, I might pick up and examine a framed picture, manicure my nails with the point of a letter opener, or flick the trigger of a cigarette lighter. In the scene I was about to play with Flynn, I idly tied and re-tied a long telephone cord.

While the lighting was being adjusted, in the hiatus between rehearsing and shooting, Raoul Walsh, the director, called me over.

"Shel, that piece of business you've got with the telephone cord...."

"Yeah."

"Don't do it."

"Why? Does it look phony?"

"No. Errol's going to do it."

The next day I found a string of beads on the set, During the rehearsal I twirled them around my forefinger. In the post rehearsal hiatus Raoul called me over.

"Hey, Shel..."

"Yeah?"

"You know that piece of business you do with the beads?"

"Yeah."

"Don't do it."

"Errol's going to do it?"

"Yeah."

From then on, I kept my hands in my pockets. Raoul asked me why I wasn't looking for some fresh business, and I told him the story of Albert and the Lion from the Yorkshire poem of that name. It tells the tale of how six-year-old Albert was taken to the zoo. He torments the caged lion until the annoyed beast retaliates by sweeping him into the cage and eating him. Albert's irate mother goes to the office of the head zoo keeper to complain. The zoo keeper refunds Albert's admission price and consoles the lady by telling her that she's a young woman and, no doubt, she can have many other children to replace Albert, to which she replies, "What! Raise more children to feed your bloody lions? Not me!"

Raoul got the point.

I remember my reunion on the set of *Tortilla Flat* with Julie Garfield, by then the solidly established star John Garfield. He enjoyed subjecting me to a lot of good natured needling relating to my prediction that he'd never make it in pictures. He invited me to dinner at his home. He wanted me to see how far he had come from the cold water flat on 23rd St.

He lived in an elegant house in Laurel Canyon and when I rang the bell, the door was opened by a butler, complete with starched shirt front and, so help me, checked vest. Cocktails were served in the library. Julie was wearing a maroon velvet smoking jacket, Robbie, his wife, was wearing a hostess gown.

There were four of us at the dinner table — Julie, Robbie, Julie's brother, and me. The table gleamed with Waterford crystal and bone china. The butler poured the wine and a white-aproned maid appeared to serve the first course. She served Robbie at the foot of the table then swung around to serve me. From the head of the table came the voice of the Lord of the Manor.

"*Schmuck!*" he roared. "You're supposed to serve from the left!"

Working on *Tortilla Flat* was a delight. Like most Metro productions, it boasted a star-studded cast. Besides Garfield there were Akim Tamiroff, Allen Jenkins, Spencer Tracy, Hedy Lamarr, and others. It was a pleasure to watch Tracy work — there was no lost motion in his performances. It was also a pleasure just to watch Lamarr, a spectacular beauty. I well remember an out-of-the-studio encounter I had with her during the filming of *Tortilla Flat*.

At the time, we had a young Mexican girl working as a mother's helper and assisting Frankie with the baby. We were horrified to learn that somewhere along the line she had acquired a severe infestation of head lice. We sent her to a dermatologist who gave her a prescription for the condition. However, she was too embarrassed to take it to the pharmacy to have it filled. I said, what the hell. I'd take it in for her.

On a day off, I took the prescription to Horton and Converse and handed it to the pharmacist. While he was studying it, in walked Hedy and her husband, John Loder. There were greetings and small talk which were interrupted by an announcement from the pharmacist as he looked up from the prescription he had been studying, "Somebody's got a nice case of lice."

I don't think my hasty explanation was accepted. For the balance of my time on the picture, Hedy never came close to me.

In *Captain Kidd*, I was playing a scar-faced, broken-nosed pirate. The part required heavy make-up, which meant a six a.m. make-up call. Laughton and John Carradine also had early make-up calls. Every morning for the next two months, with the sun not yet above the horizon, these two singularly literate actors gave a unique performance, Laughton reciting Shakespeare, Carradine reciting filthy limericks. "Oh, what a rogue and peasant slave am I", Laughton would thunder, and Carradine would respond with:

While Titian was mixing rose madder
His model ascended a ladder.
The model's position
Brought thoughts of coition
So he climbed up the ladder and had her.

Laughton's reply might be, "To be or not to be, that is the question. Whether it is nobler in the mind to suffer the slings and arrows of outrageous fortune or to take arms against the sea of troubles and by opposing, end them."
Then Carradine:

There was a young man from Capri
Who buggered an ape in a tree.
The result was quite horrid,
  Large ass and no forehead,
Three balls and a purple goatee.

When we were making *Guys and Dolls*, Frank Sinatra established himself as the host with the most. Frank enjoyed the rowdy crew that Sam Goldwyn had assembled for the picture — Stubby Kaye, Johnny Silver, B. S. Pulley, Danny Dayton, and me, not to mention Marlon Brando. Frank had a large dressing room suite. Always outrageously generous, every so often he would have a complete Italian meal flown down from his favorite Las Vegas restaurant and would invite the whole disreputable gang in for a luscious lunch.

Abbott and Costello were practical jokers. The first time I worked with them, they enlisted a nondescript character to act as a dialogue director just for my benefit. He plagued me with impossible instructions. He insisted I was doing the dialogue all wrong, and I must do it his way, because he was the dialogue director. I labored mightily to restrain my temper but there comes a time... When I was ready to kill the poor schnook, Lou Costello broke down and told me it was a joke. Then I wanted to kill him.

Both Abbott and Costello were obsessed with gambling, and they weren't very good at it. Alec Gottlieb, their producer, turned down better job offers in order to stay with Abbott and Costello because he more than doubled his salary playing gin rummy with them.

I made three pictures with Abbott and Costello. One of them, *Hit the Ice*, was set in a ski resort. A few days before production was scheduled to start, I broke my right wrist while I was playing four-wall handball with Dane Clark. He was a better player than I was and I knew it, but that only made me all the more determined to beat him. At one point, we got into a long rally. Dane could have put the ball away at any point, but he toyed with me. He popped the ball down the right side of the court, then the left side, then the right side, while I made frantic lunges from side to side to reach it. Eventually I overreached myself, I put up my hand to stop from crashing into the wall, and snap!

The orthopedist who set it called it a Colles fracture. It meant four to six weeks in a cast. I called my agent and told him that I was sorry, but he'd have to get me off the picture because I had broken my arm.

He said, "You broke your arm? That's a terrible thing to do to me!"

He was determined not to lose his ten percent. He called my orthopedist who reluctantly agreed to replace the cast on my arm with a transparent splint. With the sleeve of my ski jacket buttoned down over it, no one would know I had a broken arm — unless I tried to use it.

Okay. We started the picture and there were no problems until we came to a scene in which I was to come rushing into a room, and then, as Charlie Lamont, the director explained it, Costello was to trip me up and, as I fell, I was to grab hold of an end table for support, pulling it over and spilling a bowl of goldfish over myself.

"I can't do it, Charlie," I told him. "Give it to my stand-in."

"Come on," Charlie said. "It's an easy fall. Your grandmother could do it."

"Maybe she could, but I can't! I can't grab the table!" I peeled back my sleeve and showed him the splint. Like my agent, Charlie took it very personally. He was sure that I had broken my arm just to annoy him. Reluctantly, he put my stand-in, Paul Salta, in the shot. His job was to stand in for actors of similar height and coloring while the cameraman lit the scene, thus saving the actor hours of tedious, exhausting standing. Paul had very little experience as an actor, and he was not at ease in front of the camera when it was rolling. He came rushing into the scene, as directed. Costello tripped him. He grabbed the table as he fell. He pulled it over on himself, cracked his head open and cut himself on the broken glass from the fishbowl. Sixteen stitches. Woody VanDyke knew what he was talking about.

I did a couple of other pictures with that same director, Charles Lamont, who seemed determined to kill me. In one of them he persuaded me to forego a stunt double in a fight scene with Rod Cameron. Since Rod was going to do the fight without a double, wouldn't it be a shame if I chickened out and Charlie had to double me, thus losing the opportunity to shoot the scene nice and close? In a case like that, I always stipulated that my stunt double was to be paid to stand by and advise me on the scene. His first piece of advice was, "Don't do it."

We were on Mammoth Mountain, eight thousand feet up. The air was thin and the ground was stony, but it was too late for me to back out. Rod and I rolled around on the sharp gravel for three days of shooting, and we came out of it with very little skin intact.

But Charlie Lamont wasn't through with me.

He directed a picture I did with Gloria Jean in which I was a villainous, one-legged sea dog. To get the desired effect, the lower part of my right leg was strapped up behind me, while my flexed knee was cushioned on a wooden peg leg. It was awkward and uncomfortable and the straps had to be released frequently in order to restore circulation. The scene we were about to shoot was written to take place in a garage and we were using the actual service garage on the Universal lot. A large truck was lifted up on the hydraulic hoist which was in daily use to service the Transportation Department's vehicles.

Charlie explained the scene to me. I was to be trussed up and placed under the truck by my evil opponents. They would make it clear that if I didn't give them the information they were after they would lower the hoist, crushing me under the huge truck, and making a mess on the floor.

The hoist was operated by a switch set in the wall with up, down, and stop buttons. I would stubbornly refuse to give them the information they wanted. They would press the down button. The loaded hoist, with its deadly burden, would descend, inch by inch. Cut to a closeup of my fear-contorted face. Back to the full shot, the hoist now only inches above my helpless, writhing body. I scream in terror. I tell them what they want to know. They press the stop button.

"Let me see how it works," I said.

"No, Shel. No way," said Charlie. "It took two hours to light that damned thing. We don't want to move it until we make the shot."

"Let me see it work."

"Aw, come on! It works fine and it's late. They use this hoist every day."

"Not with trucks on it, they don't. Maybe with nice, light passenger cars. Let me see it work."

A sigh of exasperation. "Temperament, temperament! Okay, let's get on with it. Show him how it works."

The prop man pressed the down button. The loaded hoist started a shuddering descent. Down, down, down.

"Okay. Stop it."

He pressed the stop button. Nothing happened. Down, down, down until it was flat on the floor.

Charlie broke the long silence that followed.

"I guess it wasn't built to handle trucks," he said.

I remember working with Alan Ladd on *Lucky Jordan.* Alan was a courteous, considerate, kind and gentle man who made a career out of playing gangsters and gunslingers. So much for type casting. He was short, perhaps five-feet-four, but he wasn't self-conscious about his height. His wife, Sue Carol, was. She sat in on all casting sessions that concerned Alan and made sure that the people selected to play scenes with him were not taller than five-six or five-seven. When, as in my case, she was stuck with a tall actor, she stipulated that Alan was to play his scenes with me while standing on six-inch risers. Alan tolerated this sort of thing with wry amusement.

The making of *To Have and Have Not* will remain in my memory a long time, for several reasons. The director, Howard Hawks, exercised an autocratic control over his productions that was typical of a handful of top directors. He could order his producer off the set. When selecting cast or personnel, regardless of the studio's efforts to get him to use contract people, he could demand the people of his choice, whereas more mortal directors had to take what they were given. He could disregard the budget and the schedule. Here's an example.

It was a scene on the waterfront of a Caribbean island. As Humphrey Bogart emerged from a cafe, I was to fire a burst from a sub-machine gun at him from across the street. There was an ice wagon loaded with five-hundred-pound blocks of ice in the set and Mr. Hawks got the idea that it would look nice if, when I fired the sub machine gun, my bullets flicked a spray of chips from the ice cakes.

Talk about Aladdin and his magic lamp! Mr. Hawks didn't have to rub any lamp to have his wishes granted. He just had to say, "What I want is....." and the wheels would start to turn.

To get the result that Mr. Hawks wanted, the special effects man had to freeze tiny charges into the big ice blocks. He had to wire them and synchronize them with my gun so that the charges would go off when I started firing. Once started, the series of explosions couldn't be stopped.

Four hours after Mr. Hawks expressed the wish to see flying ice chips, the scene was ready. Naturally, we didn't fire the gun or blow the chips in the rehearsal, because that would have canceled a half day's work.

Everything was ready. The assistant called, "Roll 'em!"

The sound man announced "Speed!"

"Quiet, everyone!"

"Action!" Bogart came out of the cafe. I fired the gun. Ice chips flew. The gun jammed. Ice chips continued to fly.

The problem was that a fully automatic weapon is operated by recoil. Each exploding round energizes the weapon to load and fire the next round. We were not using live rounds, we were firing blanks, as required by law. Blanks have very little recoil effect, so their ability to maintain continuous firing was questionable.

Be that as it may, Mr. Hawks wants flying chips, so back to square one. Set it up for another take. The assistant announced, "It'll be a few hours, folks, so relax, everybody."

We got the shot on the fifteenth take. Two takes a day, over a period of eight working days, for a shot that lasts seven seconds on the screen.

Another thing I remember about *To Have And Have Not* is the time when Bogie first met Betty Bacall, hereafter to be called Lauren.

She was a discovery of Mr. Hawks, a lovely, unaffected Brooklyn girl, barely out of her teens, and she hit Bogie like a bolt of lightning. I suppose Bogie was in his early forties at the time but during the next few days, under the influence of Lauren's glowing youth, he regressed in behavior and demeanor by about twenty years. I think she kept him young until he died. I'm sure she kept him happy.

I remember Jimmy Stewart, just out of the army, reconditioning his long-unused acting muscles under the sensitive direction of Frank Capra during the making of *It's a Wonderful Life*. None of us could have guessed that the picture was on its way to becoming an ageless classic, perhaps on a level with *A Christmas Carol*. For the last forty years, it has flooded the airwaves every Yuletide season. It wasn't supposed to happen. Unabashed sentimentality is supposed to be out of style. I wonder, will meat and potatoes ever go out of style?

I remember darling, simple Jimmy Durante sitting in front of a table in his dressing room, staring at an array of pills he was about to take. One for his blood pressure, one for his liver, one for his kidneys, and so on. In honest bewilderment, he asked, "How do dem pills know where to go?"

Jimmy's essential simplicity sometimes transcended eloquence. One time I was discussing his choice of material with him. He explained it thus:

"I know what kinda material I like, and after all dese years, I know the kinda material dey [the audience] like. I don't do things just because I like 'em and I don't do things just because dey like 'em. I try to do things we both like."

Churchill couldn't have said it better.

As the decade of the fifties began, it became plain that change was imminent. It could be said that movies had never before been threatened by competition, but television was growing into a menacing rival. As recently as 1946, only eight percent of American homes were sampling the crude product of the young TV industry. By the middle fifties, that figure had grown to over seventy percent.

The infant television industry was spurring technical innovations that were about to make huge studio inventories of equipment obsolete. All of the major studios had backlots, often more than a hundred acres of standing sets duplicating the streets of cities all around the world. This prime real estate was being engulfed by the expanding city. As the value of the land rose spectacularly, it became unrealistic to keep this valuable asset tied up for the occasional use of a production.

Other threats to the status quo were developing. Corporate giants like Gulf + Western, TransAmerica, and MCA were looking hungrily at the studios. The government had declared the ownership of theatres by the studios a violation of the anti-trust acts. The moguls were getting older or dying off and, of all the changes, their loss would be the most damaging as the studios passed from the hands of the movie-makers into those of the deal makers.

The phenomenon that was called "Hollywood" was changing. It was becoming homogenized. By the middle fifties, doctors, lawyers, merchants, and business men outnumbered picture people in the glittering quadrangle of north Beverly Hills. Louella Parsons and Hedda Hopper, who had reigned over the picture colony as gossip columnists for many years, were being deposed. It was rumored that Louella had maintained her unshakable tenure on her job, in spite of the fact that she was barely literate, because she knew the nature of William Randolph Hearst's involvement in the mysterious disappearance of Thomas Ince, a director, who had been inexplicably lost at sea. As for Hedda,

The Stalwart Counselor (center) at Camp Wakitan, 1927.

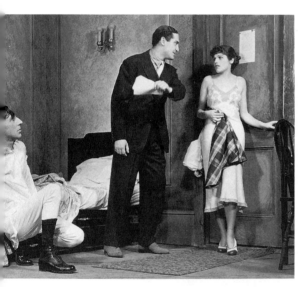

College performance of Eugene O'Neill's *Beyond the Horizon*, 1928. I'm in the center.

My first professional job— *Drums in the Night*. Shot in Jamaica in 1932.

With Percy Kilbride and Muriel Campbell in *Three Men on a Horse*, 1937.

With some of the cast of *Having Wonderful Time*. I'm in the middle, and I remember Julie (John) Garfield, who's filling his glass, and Cornel Wilde, in shirtsleeves, 1937.

An amorous moment from *Kiss the Boys Goodbye*, with Helen Claire, 1938.

My second movie, *Tall, Dark and Handsome*, 1941. I don't remember whether I was stealing Virginia Gilmore's bracelet, but I was certainly looking askance at Cesar Romero.

Hollywood made me the ultimate hoodlum, 1941.

With Judy Canova, 1943. My role on her show wasn't quite this small.

Doing my bit at the Hollywood Canteen, 1945.

Gilbert Roland, John Carradine and I, all looking daggers at Charles Laughton in *Captain Kidd*, 1945.

The Iroquois Trail, 1950. After seeing this picture, I decided not to lose my hair.

At least I was amused. On the left is cameraman Bud De Grass; on the right in Jay Sandrich, then an Assistant Director. *The Danny Thomas Show*, 1959.

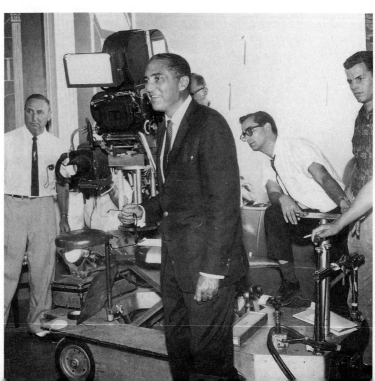

Danny Thomas shows Marjorie Lord, Hans Conried and me the architect's drawings for the St. Jude Hospital.

A gala evening with Rosemarie Thomas; Danny Thomas; my wife, Frankie; the Thomas's daughter, Terry and her friend.

I don't know why the two stars look happier than I do. Danny Thomas and
Andy Griffith and I at a dinner in 1965.

After I managed to talk CBS executives into picking up *The Dick Van Dyke Show* for a
second season, Carl Reiner and the rest of the company greeted me with this display
on my return from New York.

Leslie Caron had described their meeting this way: "She wore a hat that was big enough to shade an elephant."

No question about it, Louella and Hedda were fading. Some brave people no longer bothered to return their calls.

As film production started a steady decline, under the pressure of rising costs and increasing competition from television, the various sub-colonies started to thin out. There weren't enough jobs to justify the expensive wardrobes which the dress extras had to maintain. There weren't enough stunts to support the men who crashed cars and jumped from tall buildings. The colony of midgets who had made *The Wizard of Oz* possible felt the pinch. Yes, there was a colony of midgets.

The House UnAmerican Activities Committee did its bit toward the reduction of the creative community. It terrorized the colony. People were afraid to express their beliefs. Conversation at social events became vapidly non-controversial. Many of the most talented and sensitive artists were driven out of the community because their hatred of Fascism on the right had sent them toward the left.

I was sitting naked in the health club's sauna. I knew that the thick-shouldered, hairy-chested guy on the shelf above me had been staring at me since I came in. Few men are so secure that they can relax under close scrutiny when naked. I am not one of those few, so I was pleased when Hairy Chest exited shortly after I came in.

When I was sufficiently broiled, I showered and started to dress. Terry Hunt, the owner of the club, came over to my locker with Hairy Chest.

"Sheldon Leonard," he said. "I want you to meet Detective Sergeant Levinson of the Beverly Hills Police Force."

"Glad to know you, Sergeant."

"Not as glad as I am to know you," he replied. "Terry just saved me from making a horse's ass of myself."

"How's that?"

"I was just going to phone in for a surveillance team to keep an eye on you, because you looked to me like someone who was hot somewhere. I figured I must have seen your kisser on a wanted flyer, but when Terry told me who you were, I realized I must have seen you in one of them gangster pictures."

It was time for my career to change direction. I had been pushed back into the type-casting rut again. With fewer movies being made, it had become difficult for me to be choosy about the parts I played. As a provider, I had to work, so I was back to being suave and villainous again.

Picture production had been falling off since the beginning of the fifties. Since double-bills were disappearing, the first to go were the "B"s, their low-budget bottom halves. The emphasis was on spectacles, because television's small screen couldn't compete in that area. The studios were making big musicals, costume epics, and historicals. There wasn't much in them for me.

I remembered a scene in Harriet Beecher Stowe's novel, *Uncle Tom's Cabin*. Eliza, an escaping slave, eludes the pursuing bloodhounds by leaping from one floe to another as she crosses the icy Ohio River. I was beginning to feel like Eliza. Pursued by unemployment, I had jumped from the sinking ice floe of the legitimate theatre to the greater security of motion pictures. Now it was time to jump again. For me, the next ice floe was called radio.

Surveys had shown that radio in the forties had replaced movies as the principal form of leisure entertainment, with an astonishing average of five-and-a-half listening hours a day in the ninety-eight per cent of American homes that had radios. This enormous audience made its size felt in a variety of ways. When *Amos 'n' Andy*, or any other popular program was on the air, street traffic slowed to a trickle. Restaurants were empty. The water companies could tell when the commercials were on, because the consumption of water multiplied as toilets from coast to coast were being flushed.

Prime time radio was divided among three cities, New York, Chicago, and Los Angeles. New York had the prestige broadcasts, such as Arturo Toscanini and the Philharmonic, Dr. Walter Damrosch and his seminars on music appreciation, and the Metropolitan Opera. Several dramatic anthologies and daytime serials — called "soap operas," because they were sponsored by soap and detergent companies wanting to reach the housewife engaged in her daily chores — were broadcast from Chicago. Los Angeles had all the major comedy shows, with the exception of Fred

Allen, who could not be pried away from his New York habitat.

The NBC studios in Hollywood were at the corner of Sunset and Vine. CBS was at Sunset and Gower. It was three hundred and sixty paces from the side door at NBC to its counterpart at CBS. It took two and three-quarter minutes to negotiate that distance at a moderate pace, so as not to arrive breathless. This proximity was important to the small colony of actors who commanded pay that was higher than union scale, a tight little group consisting of Mel Blanc, Hans Conried, Elliot Lewis, Bea Benaderet, Sandra Gould, myself and a couple of dozen others. Elite members of this group were often offered conflicting assignments, like *The Jack Benny Show* at CBS and *The Phil Harris Show* at NBC. If the actor could get a look at the conflicting scripts, and, by timing them out, determine that he spoke his last lines on the *Benny* show twelve minutes and forty-four seconds into the broadcast, and didn't speak on the *Harris* show until fifteen minutes and fifty-six seconds, he would know he had three minutes and twelve seconds — plenty of time to get from one to the other, and could pick up both checks. This kind of split-second timing was possible because radio was run by the stopwatch.

Comedy shows were the big, juicy plums for actors. They paid well over scale, and if you were hot, you could do two, three, or even four of them on a given Sunday. It was nice, clean, easy work. You appeared in the morning and read the script around the table, for timing. Then you had time off, while the writers made their cuts and revisions. You came back for a final reading on mike before air time, did the broadcast, and went home to wait for your check. Since I had established a fee of three hundred fifty dollars per broadcast, I was on my way to becoming a goddam plutocrat.

I had things neatly organized, so I could do a *Jack Benny* reading during the break of the *Maisie* show, then, with any luck, work an *Amos 'n' Andy* into the gaps. On other days, I did *The Judy Canova Show, Bob Hope, Phil Harris,* and *Edgar Bergen* on a more or less regular basis, along with whatever else I could pick up. It was Fat City.

All of those shows were performed before an audience, and there has never been a better school for developing comedy timing, that mysterious skill which enables a performer to get the maximum laugh value out of a line or a situation. It is not a natural gift, nor is it a teachable skill. It is something that is acquired by bouncing comedy off thousands of audiences. It is pure pragmatism.

The biggest mistake a performer can make, when he sets out to entertain audiences, is to believe that they share his sense of humor. He will live or die by what *they* think is funny, not by what he thinks.

The ex-vaudevillians, Jack Benny, Bob Hope, Burns and Allen, Edgar Bergen, and their contemporaries came into radio endowed with comedy timing earned by exposure to four or five audiences a day. Audiences at every age level, with every sort of religious, ethnic, or educational background, had told them, by their laughter, what they thought was funny. After a while, they learned, with inbred certainty, when to expect a laugh and how to feed it. That was an indispensable skill when playing radio shows in front of an audience. If the actor couldn't sense when a laugh was coming, he was liable to step in to it, smothering his dialogue in the laugh. When that happened a few times, the audience was likely to stop laughing for fear that they might miss what was being said.

The audience radio shows of the fifties were uniquely valuable to the actors who worked them, because vaudeville had disappeared, stock and repertory were gone, there were no more road shows, no burlesque, no Chautauqua, nowhere to get the irreplaceable benefit of exposure to audiences. When you put several hundred people together in an audience, the comedy values change. Tell a joke to a man on the street and you may be rewarded with a chuckle. Tell the same joke to a luncheon gathering of fifty and you'll get a laugh. Tell it to five hundred people in an auditorium and you'll get a roar.

The vaudevillians had an almost magical ability to multiply the value of a laugh, to milk it, to feed it, and to control it. There is a story that has become a legend, about how Jack Benny worked what may have been the longest laugh in radio history.

(There are some who claim that the longest laugh in radio history came when an eagle escaped from his trainer on *The Fred Allen Show*, flew up into the eaves, and dropped a souvenir on the stage. Fred ad libbed, "Oh, a critic!" and got a monstrous laugh. However, since it wasn't in the script, I don't think it should qualify for the record.)

Going back to Jack's big laugh, here's how it happened.

Jack is approaching his home by way of a darkened side street. A masked man steps out from behind a shrub and demands, "Your money or your life."

Jack stares at the mugger and, of course, the audience starts to laugh. Jack turns his head and stares at the audience. The laugh grows. He turns back to the mugger, indecision written on his face. The laugh is now a roar. The holdup man says, "Quit stalling! Your money or your life!"

Jack says, "I'M THINKING! I'M THINKING!" Pandemonium!

The leading radio comics had very different styles. Jack's comedy depended on character, and he protected the integrity of his synthesized character to the degree that the real Jack Benny disappeared, to be replaced by a fiction. Generous, modest, shy Benny Kubelsky didn't exist in the public mind. They only knew arrogant, vain, stingy Jack Benny.

Milt Josefsberg, one of Jack's writers, got a long distance call. The operator announced that it was "Person to Person to Mr. Milt Josefsberg from Mr. Jack Benny, only I don't think it's really him because he didn't call collect."

I asked Jack about his use of the word "well," which he employed with various shadings of frustration, indignation, indecision, etc, and which always got a laugh.

"What's funny about the word 'well'?" I asked.

"I don't know," he replied. "Ask *them*."

He didn't know why they laughed, but he knew they would, with a knowledge based on layer after layer of experience. His response to their laughter was reflexive. That's timing.

Jack was a fine editor, and he worked very closely with his writers. His was the final word as to what was right or wrong for his character. For example, he had a very funny routine in which he described meeting a beautiful, seductive lady in a bar. After a few drinks, she suggested that they retire to the privacy of her room. Being lonely, he accepted her invitation. Once there he waited while she changed into something more comfortable. She emerged in a flimsy negligee, started a record player, and held out her arms in an invitation to dance. Her lips came closer and closer to Jack's. As they were about to touch she swept off her wig and cried, "I'm Allen Funt! Smile, you're on *Candid Camera*!" The punch line of the routine was Jack saying. "I was so surprised I could hardly finish the dance!"

George Burns offered Jack a funnier punch line. He was to say, "I wasn't too disappointed, because I saved fifty dollars." Everybody agreed that it was a funnier line than the one he had been using, but Jack turned it down. He said, quite correctly, that the line was inconsistent with his scrupulously maintained character. It made him out to be a dirty old man instead of a *schnook*.

Jack was an enthusiastic straight man for all the members of his cast — for Mel Blanc, Dennis Day, Phil Harris, Frank Nelson, Mary Livingston, Rochester (Eddie Anderson), and me. He would set up the jokes for us with matchless technique, and nobody enjoyed the laughs we got at his expense more than he did.

George Burns was another superb straight man, but only for Gracie. George was a first-class comedy writer and editor, and he devoted himself to the character he had created for his wife. His deadpan acceptances of her lunacies was a major reason for the success of her zany character.

Bob Hope hasn't ever bothered with character very much. He has a rapid-fire delivery and excellent timing, so his writers just give him a lot of jokes and a free rein. In his opening monologue, he uses many more jokes and one-liners than the time spot can possibly contain. He rattles them off, one after the other. The ones that get the biggest laughs are retained, the others are cut. It is survival of the fittest.

W.C. Fields, in person, was not very different from the character he portrayed on radio. He was a gruff, bibulous freewheeler. An authenticated story about an episode that occurred when he was starring in *The Ziegfeld Follies* on Broadway tells a lot about him.

He was a proficient juggler. Part of his act consisted of juggling several pool balls and a pool cue. One night he was puzzled because he was getting laughs in spots where he had never gotten them before. He looked down to see Eddie Cantor's head sticking out from under the pool table. Cantor was mugging away a mile a minute. Fields belted Eddie over the head with his pool cue, knocking him cold, and went on with his routine. The audience loved it — they thought it was part of the act. The management wanted to keep it in but, for some reason, Eddie wouldn't agree.

On radio, Fields pulled a beautiful scam on his sponsor, Camel cigarettes. He carried it on for months.

Cigarette sponsors were paranoid about plugging competitive brands on the air time they had paid for. If the show was sponsored by Camels, you could say someone was fortunate, but you could not say that he was lucky. Similarly, if Lucky Strikes was the sponsor, and the script referred to Arabs, they supposedly rode in on horses, never on camels.

Over a period of time, in a program sponsored by Camels, W.C. Fields had made many references on the air to his son, Chester. Imagine the corporate dismay when some alert Camel executive realized that the son's full name had to be Chester Fields!

Most of the radio comics realized and acknowledged their dependence on their writers, but there were those who would have liked the public to believe that they had made up all the funny stuff themselves. When Red Skelton was asked how he got the ideas for his routines, he answered, "I don't know. I just get up to perform and God tells me what to do." When Red's writers took offense at this and asked for some credit, he accused them of being "...so egotistical that they wanted credit over God."

The radio stars and their writers were hard workers. They had to create, polish and perform a new show every week. That was a very demanding job, then without precedent in the history of show business. Most entertainment, from a vaudeville act to a circus, was designed to be used for a season or more, but this voracious new medium gobbled up material at an unprecedented rate. It was easy to complain about the mediocrity of the stuff on the air, but nobody ever asked Rembrandt to come up with a new masterpiece every week. Considering the volume of material they had to come up with and the ever-present threat of a deadline, I think the radio writers did a pretty good job.

They were also a colorful lot, their ranks containing more than the normal percentage of exotics and zanies. There were people like John Tackaberry, one of Benny's writers, a bone-deep Texan in word and manner. He tried hard to overcome the prejudice against Jews and blacks that was a part of his regional heritage. Tack was very proud of the way he put down a bigot who was mouthing anti-Semitic remarks in his presence. He reported to his fellow writers that he had said, "Now listen here! I make my living writing for Jack Benny and Rochester and I'm here to tell you that I never met two finer people, so I don't want to hear no more nasty remarks about niggers and kikes!"

There was Artie Stander who, when Zsa Zsa Gabor complained about a facelift joke in her guest spot, told her, "Zsa Zsa, one more facelift and you'll have pubic hair on your chin."

Artie was part of another episode that became legendary among radio writers. At the time he was collaborating with another comedy writer, Fat Larry Marks. (There was also a comedy writer called Thin Larry Marks.) It seems that Artie and Fat Larry took from the same psychoanalyst, Dr. Jud Marmor. Every day, Fat Larry saw him at eleven A.M., while Artie had a four P.M. appointment. They commented on Dr. Marmor's imperturbability — no matter what they told him, he never turned a hair. Nothing seemed to surprise him or disturb him. They decided to shake him up.

They made up a dream, full of Freudian implications and exotic sexual occurrences. At eleven a.m., Fat Larry recited their invention to Dr. Marmor. At four p.m., Artie recited the same scenario. Dr. Marmor reacted with appropriate astonishment.

"This is astounding, Artie!" he exclaimed. "I've never heard of anything like it! It's unbelievable! You are the third person today who has told me the same dream!"

Hal Kanter once described writer Sid Dorfman as "...such a gourmet that he stopped speaking to his producer for weeks, because the guy had drunk white wine after chewing his ass out."

Harry Crane who, at one time or another was a head writer for most of the radio comics, had a luncheon date with Joey Bishop. They were to meet at Nate 'n Al's delicatessen and Harry got there early. He is a diabetic, and as he waited for Joey he felt the onset of an attack of hypoglycemia, a hazard that results from an insulin overdose that danger-ously depletes the blood sugar. To abort the attack, the victim must get sugar into his system in some form — a piece of chocolate, a lump of sugar, a piece of fruit.

As the vertigo and nausea increased, Harry made his way to the deli counter and asked the counterman, "Please give me an orange."

"It's not your turn," the counterman replied. "Take a ticket."

"No. I can't wait. I've got to have it now."

"Everybody's in a hurry! There are people ahead of you. Relax. Take a table. Have a regular lunch, not just a piece of fruit. It's not good for you."

"Please! I need it now...." and that was as far as he got before he passed out.

The paramedics came and took him to Midway Hos-pital, just outside of Beverly Hills. They deposited him in the Emergency Room where his condition was quickly diag-nosed and steps were taken to correct it.

Meanwhile, Joey Bishop had arrived at Nate 'n Al's.

"I was supposed to meet Harry Crane here," he told the cashier.

"Harry was here already," she replied. "He passed out. They took him to the hospital."

"For God's sake! What hospital?"

"Midway."

Joey got on the phone to Midway Hospital. They put him through to the room where Harry was recovering.

"Harry! What happened?"

"I passed out."

"Are you all right now?"

"I'll be fine."

"Look, I'm coming over to see you. Midway Hospital? How do you get there?"

"You go to Nate 'n Al's and you ask for an orange."

George Burns's brother, Willie, was on his writing staff, teamed with Artie Phillips. They had a long-term social relationship outside of working hours. Their wives were part of a regular foursome for dinner and bridge, which gave the boys a weekly opportunity to go alley catting, providing they were ready to pick up their spouses when the bridge game ended around eleven-thirty.

One week, their adventure was going according to plan, starting in a swinging singles bar and winding up in the apartment of the two girls they had met there. The evening grew late. When Artie looked at his watch, glowing in the darkened room, he let out a yell.

"Hey, Willie! For God's sake! It's after eleven!"

They scrambled into their clothes and rushed to pick up their wives.

The women were in the coffee and cake stage of the evening when Willie and Artie burst in on them. Artie's wife, Charlotte, looked up and exclaimed, "Look at you guys! You're wearing Willie's pants and he's wearing yours!"

Displaying the ingenuity that characterized his writing, Artie said, "We were shacked up with a couple of girls we met in a bar and we got dressed in the dark, so I guess we got our pants mixed up."

Charlotte dismissed them with, "Oh, you two wise guys! Some joke. Get out of here!"

Milt Josefberg, later to become Lucille Ball's head writer, was part of a group of radio people I invited down to Baja California annually for a week of fishing. He knocked on the door of my *casita* at seven one morning with this plaintive request, "My roommate is constipated. Can I borrow a cup of shit?"

The institution of "the plug" was a unique part of radio. "Schlockmeisters" was a less than affectionate term for those who dispensed goodies to radio writers in exchange for on-the-air mentions of the products they represented.

For instance, if the dialogue went like this, "I thought I was late, so I looked at my Bulova...." that was worth a case of Scotch for the writers. "I pedaled up the hill on my Schwinn bicycle...." brought a case of Mumm's Cordon Rouge.

Plugs for Bendix washing machines, Old Grandad whiskey, Admiral radios, and many other products were good for a variety of benefits, including round-trip plane tickets to a destination of your choice. Even such innocuous mentions as, "We went bowling and it was fun," or "The lamb was delicious," would be rewarded with whiskey, wrist watches, portable radios or whatever, by the grateful promoters of the sport of bowling or the marketing of lamb. One leading comic hit a bonanza by reading, on the air, his list of Christmas gifts for cast and crew: twenty-nine plugs in one swoop.

A bit of dialogue on one *Jack Benny Show* went like this:

ROCHESTER
Boss, it's chilly out. Want me to turn up the heat?

JACK
No. Just turn up my General Electric blanket.

ROCHESTER
But, Boss, you don't have a General Electric
blanket.

JACK

I do now.

Radio was nice easy work — no lines to memorize, no early makeup calls, no distant locations. In fact, it was too easy. Most of my work was done on two or, at most, three days in the week. That left me with a lot of time to get in trouble. The town was full of seductions. There were two beautiful racetracks nearby, beaches, bars, gin rummy games at the Health Club, and Las Vegas only an hour away. I never claimed to be immune to temptation.

Let me say in passing the problem I am describing is the reason for much of the exotic behavior that is attributed to the people in the entertainment industry. Too much money, too much opportunity, and too much leisure.

I chose to keep out of mischief by writing. I wrote a couple of scripts for pictures, and — what do you know? — people bought them! I turned my hand to radio scripts, because half-hour playlets were very much in demand for anthology shows like *Broadway Is My Beat*. Scripts were bought as fast as I could turn them out. Writing, it seemed, was not only therapeutic and prophylactic, but profitable as well.

The entertainment climate was changing as the mid-fifties approached. Big-time radio was fading and television was fast emerging.

Look! Here comes another ice floe!

six

Action...Cut!

In the early days of television, the anthology shows were starving for scripts. This was understandable because they paid a pittance for their material. Rudy Abel, a friend of mine, was producing a TV show called *The Jewelers' Showcase*. Knowing that rights to the material I had sold to radio had reverted to me after broadcast, he persuaded me to adapt it to TV.

It was easy to do. For instance, a line written for radio might go like this:

TOM
I'm going to turn off the lights. [SOUND EFFECT: Light switch clicks.]

For video it was simply: Tom flicks off light switch.

For radio:

TOM
Let me pour you a drink. [SOUND EFFECT: Gurgle of liquid pouring.]

For video: Tom pours a drink.

Otherwise, dialogue, character, and story line remained the same.

Because of my rapidly developing affluence, I didn't balk at selling my first half-hour teleplays for the giveaway price of three hundred dollars. Although the price was beggarly, the benefits of those sales proved to be enormous. They opened the door to directing, and to creating and producing series programming for television.

I had written one radio script with a juicy part in it for myself. It was based on a famous California homicide case, in which a woman and her paramour murdered her parents for their money. The woman was tried for murder, and with the help of a brilliant lawyer and an array of technicalities, she beat the rap. The jury found her "not guilty."

Her lover had not been indicted and consequently he had not been brought to trial. Since the woman had been tried and judged not guilty, she was for evermore in the clear. According to the laws against double jeopardy, she could never be tried again for the same offense. But her partner was still vulnerable.

She could, if she chose, testify against him, thus assuring his conviction, without endangering herself.

This situation leads to a steadily mounting level of tension between the two murderers. He knows that she can send him to death row; and she knows that he can correct the situation by getting rid of her.

I adapted the script for television and sold it to Rudy Abel with the stipulation that I was to play the man. After the picture was shot, I wormed my way into the editing room to see the rough cut. I was aghast at what I saw. The director had succeeded in missing every significant moment.

"Haven't you got a close up of her when she starts to cry?"

The editor said, "Nope. Wish we had one."

"Why is the camera on my back when I'm making the decision to kill her? Haven't you got something on my face?"

"Nope. That's the way he shot it."

I went to Rudy's office, and recited the poem about Albert and the Lion.

"We do the best we can," he told me. "Our budget is very tight. We can't afford Guild directors. We take what we can get."

I wasn't satisfied with that answer. I kept on complaining. I realized that I had painted myself into a corner when Rudy said, "If that's the way you feel about it, why don't you try directing one? Let's see how you make out."

I went to the offices of the Directors Guild of America, paid the initiation fee, phoned my wife and said, "Hey, honey, what do you know? I'm a director!"

I approached my first day as a motion picture director with the reassuring knowledge that the skilled professionals behind the camera wouldn't let me make any serious mistakes. My head cameraman was a distinguished craftsman, James (Jimmy) Wong Howe, who, besides being a fine cinematographer, ran an excellent Chinese restaurant, on busy Ventura Boulevard in the Valley. He once told me about preparing for the restaurant's gala opening, with many of the celebrities he had photographed scheduled to attend. He noticed a photographer from the *Valley Times* setting up to record the event. The poor guy was having a bad time. In order to get the whole elaborate facade of the restaurant in the shot, he had to back his camera into the heavy traffic of Ventura Boulevard. As he attempted to set up, cars whipped by, each near miss making him flinch.

Jimmy watched for a while. Then he approached the frazzled man and said, "You know, if you snap on a wide angle lens, you can move your camera up on the sidewalk."

The photographer gave him a disdainful look and said, "Look, Chinaman, let me take the pictures and you go cook your noodles."

I resolved that if Jimmy ever offered me a bit of advice I would not tell him to go cook his noodles. The same held true for the sound man, the electricians, the prop men, the special effects men, or any of the army of skilled technicians, all of whom knew a hell of a lot more about picture making than I did.

A director doesn't have to be an expert in all the technical aspects of film making, though a smattering of knowledge doesn't hurt. He does have to surround himself with people who are expert, and he must have the good sense to accept their help. His attention is better focused on what's happening in front of the camera and in the editing room.

A good editor can work wonders with a film. He can control the pace of a scene, and determine where to put the emphasis. He can heighten suspense, intensify drama, turn a mediocre picture into a good one, and a good picture into an excellent one.

A good director is not unlike the conductor of an orchestra. He controls tempo, tone, piano, fortissimo. He corrects mistakes.

My first shot as a director was a master scene, in a script I had written. Involving five actors, it required moderately complicated staging, with correspondingly complicated camera moves. I staged the scene, rehearsed it, and made some minor changes in the dialogue. Then I turned it over to the stand-ins and the camera and sound people.

When everything was ready, the assistant director got the actors in place, called for silence on the set, and gave the command to roll the cameras. The sound man announced "Speed." The slate man clapped his sticks together, announced the number of the scene, and cleared the set. Silence descended. Seconds passed. Why was nothing happening? Why didn't someone say "Action!"? Why was everybody looking at me?

When I belatedly pulled myself together and said the magic word, the scene started to play. What do you know? I was a director!

Things went quite smoothly after that, until I came to a scene between J. Carrol Naish and Giselle Werbiscek Piffle.

That's right. Giselle Werbiscek Piffle. She was a charming lady in her eighties, a refugee from Eastern Europe, who had been a major star in the Hungarian theatre.

Her name had created a unique problem for her. She had been harassed by a series of anonymous phone calls that went something like this: "Hello. Is this Giselle Werbiscek Piffle?"

"Yes."

"Your golf clubs are ready. You can pick them up any time."

"Golf clubs? I don't know from golf clubs."

"You don't?"

"No."

"It must be some other Giselle Werbiscek Piffle." Then he'd hang up.

The poor lady had her phone number changed several times, but the caller always found her. Finally, she paid for an unlisted number.

In the scene she was to play with Naish, they were an elderly couple celebrating their fiftieth wedding anniversary when they learn that the minister who performed their wedding ceremony half a century before was a fraud. Their marriage is not legal. Their five children are bastards.

Their disenfranchised children are frantically eager to see their parents remarried legally. However, the old lady demands a proper proposal, such as she was denied when her parents arranged the marriage fifty years ago. No proposal, no marriage. Eighty-four-year-old Naish gets down on one knee to vow eternal love for eighty-year-old Giselle, and to ask for her hand in marriage. It should have been a charming scene, right? Except that the goddam actor was hoot-owl drunk. No way he could remember his lines.

I couldn't send him home to sober up, because another company was waiting to use the set as soon as I got my scene. A more experienced director could have handled the problem in one of several ways. He could have shot Giselle's closeups, and gotten Naish's at a later date in front of a neutral background. He could have put a stand-in in the scene and shot it over his shoulder, laying in Naish's dialogue later.

I chose to record his dialogue, sound only, one line at a time, between giving him slugs of black coffee. Then I played the whole scene over Giselle's lovely, seamed face, her eyes wet with tears, as she reacted to the fulfillment of her long-held dream. You never saw the drunken son of a bitch. It worked just fine. It made a lovely scene.

Yes, an experienced director might have handled it differently, but it was hard to get good directors to work in television. The pay was poor, about twenty percent of the prevailing rates at the picture studios, and it was hard work. A TV director was expected to shoot from ten to fifteen script pages a day. Four pages was a good day's work at the majors. Most important, directors who worked in TV were endangering their careers in pictures. The studios had come to recognize the threat posed by the newcomer, and they didn't look kindly on anyone who contributed to it.

That was okay with me. I wasn't interested in making theatrical pictures. I believed in the future of television. I had been a part of the last glory days of legit. I had been on board when the picture industry started to founder. I had felt radio slipping out from under my feet. I had my fill of trying to stay even in declining fields of the entertainment industry. Now I was in a part of show business that was on the way up. It felt good.

The giant William Morris Agency also saw television as the hope for the future, and the networks were starving for comedy shows. The agency had a long list of performers with whom to meet that demand, but they were short of comedy directors. Norman Brokaw, a bright, ambitious young man, fresh from an apprenticeship in the mail room, recruited me. A protégé of Abe Lastfogel, the president of the Morris Agency, he was destined to follow in Mr. Lastfogel's footsteps, becoming president of the agency in the eighties. Along the way, Norman guided the careers of ex-presidents, Olympic athletes, actors, writers, and even a racehorse. (He represented Secretariat.)

A few days after I signed with him, he put me together with Danny Thomas. Danny wasn't too happy about the arrangement. Years later, Norman told me that when he proposed me as Danny's director, Danny said, "You mean to say you're going to let me be directed by an actor? Worse yet, a gangster-type actor! No way! Get me a regular director."

For the first few months of the show Danny was testing me. It became more and more awkward until one day I said, "We can only have one director on this show. If you want to be it, okay." I walked off the set. Immediately, Danny panicked and came after me. It wasn't long after that we realized what a felicitous pairing we were.

The Morris office had offered a package to the ABC Network consisting of Ray Bolger in a half-hour show with music and dancing, and Danny Thomas in a situation comedy about the home life of an entertainer, to be called *Make Room for Daddy*. The network wanted Bolger, but they weren't crazy about Danny. Mr. Lastfogel, dealing from strength, stipulated that it was both or none. Both shows went on. Bolger was canceled after his second season, Danny stayed on the air for eleven years. Later, I will provide other examples of the flawless judgment of network program executives.

Make Room for Daddy was produced with a technique pioneered by Desi Arnaz for the *Lucy* show. Operating on the well-founded belief that a comedy show needs an audience to give it the authentic response that canned laughter can never duplicate, Desi brought in an audience to watch and react, while he used a multiple-camera shooting technique borrowed from live TV. Traditionally, films were shot with a single camera, re-set for different angles. Live shows used three or four video cameras at the same time, to give the director a choice of shots.

Our multiple-camera system had many advantages. It gave us a choice of camera angles for the film editor to work with, and it gave us some control over the length of each episode. We had to deliver precisely twenty-six minutes and twenty seconds of film to the network; the thirty-minute spot was filled out with commercials and credits. In live TV, the director exercised some sort of control over length with hand signals given by the stage manager. He could speed up the action by making a rapid, circular motion with his forefinger, or slow down the tempo by pulling his hands apart.

Control of length was particularly difficult on comedy shows. If the audience liked a show, their laughter could cause three or four minutes of spread. If they liked it very much, you might spread as much as six minutes. We could exert a great deal of control over the length of an episode in the cutting room, tightening shots, trimming speeches, and even cutting whole scenes.

We were contracted to deliver thirty-nine new episodes per season. It was a tough schedule. More than nineteen hours of material conceived, written, rehearsed, performed, edited, scored and delivered. That's a lot. Bear in mind that, in a single season, a half-hour sitcom series consumes enough script material for ten feature pictures.

Each episode had a four-day schedule. The camera and sound crews didn't come in until the third day, which gave me two days with the cast, to work on the script and rehearse.

We spent the first day sitting around the table, revising, sharpening, editing, and polishing the scripts. If we did a good job on that first day, the rest came easily.

The second rehearsal day was for staging. Television directors didn't have many opportunities to reshape characterizations or change readings, because by the second or third episodes the characters were set in concrete.

The third day was a blocking day. The cameramen came, and we set up the shots. "Camera One, you go to your next mark when Danny moves. Camera Two, you take your cue to move from Jean's speech. Camera Three...."

The fourth day was spent polishing and refining camera moves, readings, and business. The audience would be admitted at seven o'clock, whereupon Danny would spend a half hour or so warming them up, getting them in a mood to laugh freely. By seven-forty-five, we were ready to roll. Barring problems, by nine-thirty the show was in the can, and Danny had his makeup off. He, his wife, Rosemarie, my wife and I, and maybe one or two other cast members were on our way to a well-earned Italian dinner — for which Danny invariably picked up the check. Well, what the hell, he was our boss, and *noblesse oblige*, right?

The time spent around the table on the first day was the most important part of the preparation for each episode. The scripts, which needed a lot of fixing, were the product of many talented writers, who were doing their best to meet the demands of a medium that chewed up enormous amounts of material every week. Historically, plays were tried out out of town and then revised. Pictures were sneak-previewed in obscure theatres, then re-cut or re-shot. TV didn't have the luxury of a tryout. We had to call on our experience and our instincts to get it right the first time around.

Most of the comedy writers had gained their experience writing for radio. They had written jokes for Hope, Benny, Berle, and others. They were not experienced in situation comedy, and we sought to get laughs from the situation, not from jokes. Our scripts had to be credible. Hope could start a comedy sequence with, "Well, here we are in darkest Africa." We couldn't. His scripts could jump from sketches to musical numbers. Ours had to have a beginning, a middle, and an end.

Danny's extraordinary awareness of audiences was of great value around the table. If he complained about a line, or a scene, or even the whole premise, it was unwise to disregard that complaint just because he couldn't be specific. We would examine and pick at the subject until we found what was wrong with it. Then we'd fix it.

At one time or another, many fine comedy writers assisted in the literary surgery we performed around the table. Milt Josefsberg, fresh from *The Jack Benny Show*, was with us for many years. Danny Simon, the older brother Neil Simon dramatized in many of his plays, did time with us.

And then there was Artie Stander. You've read about him before, but he was an inexhaustible source of anecdotal material. He was a character. He was short, about five-feet-four, and that fact shaped his personality. He was pugnacious, aggressive, and competitive. Nobody was going to push him around just because he was short! "I could have been tall," he claimed, "but I turned it down."

Among the many stories circulating industry-wide about Artie's feistiness is one that dates back to when he was collaborating with Charlie Isaacs on *The Joan Davis Show*. Charlie was a pacer. He would stride back and forth, wearing a path in the carpet, while he threw lines at Artie. Artie, seated at the typewriter, would make tentative selections from the flood of material and type them out. Every once in a while, Charlie, loaded with excess energy, would interrupt his pacing to spring high in the air and flick the ceiling with his fingertips. Then he would resume pacing and composing dialogue. After one such leap, he became aware that Artie had stopped typing. He turned to him.

"What's the matter?"

A brief silence, then: "I can do that."
"Do what?"
"Jump up and touch the ceiling. I can do it."
"Sure. Nobody said you couldn't"
"But you don't believe I can do it. Right?"
"Sure I do."
"No, you don't, but I'll show you."
Artie came out from behind the typewriter, and took a position in the middle of the room. "Just because I don't go leaping around like a goddam kangaroo don't mean I can't do it."
"Sure. Sure."
"Just watch."
He gathered himself together and jumped. He came up an inch or two short. "Just warming up," he announced.
A few deep breaths, then a leap and another miss. Then a muttered curse, and another futile jump. Again, and yet again, and as the margin of failure became wider with each attempt, it became evident, even to Artie, that he wasn't going to make it. Finally accepting the inevitable, he turned to Charlie and grumbled, "Well, you don't smoke!"
In the third year of Artie's tenure with us, I took *Make Room for Daddy* to Europe, to get it away from the confines of Stage Five and open it up. I scheduled episodes in England, Ireland, France, and Italy. I brought Artie along to adapt the scripts to whatever conditions we found on the locations.
When we worked in Paris, it became customary to get together for a before-dinner drink. We had learned early that the maitre d's of such fine restaurants as Maxim's, Tour D'Argent, or LaSerre did not look kindly on guests who drank hard liquor before dinner. Vermouth or other mild aperitifs were okay, but Martinis and the like were supposed to dull the palate, preventing full appreciation of the gourmet menu. In order to avoid the withering stares of the various maitre d's, Danny and Rosemarie and Artie and his

lady would join Frankie and me in our apartment at the
George V, where we would proceed to dull our palates as
much as we wished.

On one occasion, Artie and Joan were quite late. Tardiness is unusual among show people. You have to be there
when the curtain goes up, or when the "On The Air" light
goes on, so we were a little concerned. When the couple
finally showed up, I asked, "What happened?"

Joan started to giggle uncontrollably.

"Cut it out!" Artie snarled, but that only turned her
giggles into laughter.

"What's going on?" I wanted to know.

"Nothing. She's just being silly."

More laughter.

Artie surrendered. "Oh, hell! Go ahead. Tell them."

"We were late because I had to put on a whole new
face. Artie made me laugh so hard that I cried, and my
makeup ran."

"Why? How?"

"I went into the bathroom, and I saw Artie standing
on the toilet, peeing, not in front of the toilet, on it. Way up
in the air, peeing down."

More laughter. When she regained control: "I said,
'Artie, what are you doing up there?' and he said...." Giggle,
giggle, giggle.... "He said, 'I just wanted to see what it felt
like to be Gary Cooper.'"

I found working on foreign locations immensely stimulating. Making pictures in a studio environment can be very
demanding, but one seldom has to deal with the unexpected.
On foreign locations, the unexpected is the rule. Writers sit
at their typewriters in Hollywood and write a nice little scene
to be played on a balcony overlooking the Piazza Navona
with its lovely Bernini fountains. When you get to Rome, you
discover that there are no balconies overlooking the Piazza

Navona. So, you improvise. Sometimes you come out a winner, and sometimes you don't.

Once, we were set up in the Hotel Bauer Grunwald in Venice, in a gorgeous suite overlooking the Grand Canal. The scene we were about to shoot called for Danny and Marjorie (Maggie) Lord, playing Mr. and Mrs. Danny Williams, to be led into the suite by Piccola Pupa, which means "little doll" in Italian. Pupa was a precocious ten-year-old girl we had auditioned in Rome, who could belt out a song like crazy and act up a storm. Pupa would lead the couple to the window and, pointing to a gondola in the canal below, would say, "The gondolier. He is my papa. He sings very good. Sing for Mr. Williams, Papa. Sing!"

We discover that her purpose is to get Danny Williams, the famous American entertainer, to bring Papa to America, and make him a star.

When we were ready to shoot the scene, what happened was typical of what can be expected when you venture out from the shelter of studio walls. The grips had been setting up lights and sound equipment since early morning. A big generator was humming on a barge tied up to the hotel's dock. Cables had been strung from the generator to the windows of our suite. The cameras were ready. The scene had been rehearsed. We were set to roll, when the hotel manager burst into the suite.

"Out! Out! Everybody out!" he shouted.

"What goes on? You gave us permission to shoot in this apartment."

"I didn't know you were going to make my beautiful hotel ugly with all those cables! Those terrible cables, all over the front of my building!"

Our Italian Unit Manager, Danilo Sabatini, was equal to the situation. He grabbed the manager by the arm. "Come to your office, where we can talk about it quietly," he said, half leading him, half shoving him out the door. I knew I could count on him to keep the manager occupied long enough for me to get the shot.

We sprang into action. The camera rolled, and I started the scene. Piccola Pupa led Danny and Maggie into the suite. They marveled at its elegance. Pupa led them to the window. She pointed to Papa. "Sing, Papa. Sing!" she commanded.

Nothing.

Cut!

"What's the matter? That was his cue. Why doesn't he sing?"

A rattle of Italian between the gondolier and our interpreter.

The interpreter finally explained, "He says he can't sing, because the other gondoliers make fun of him. They ask him if he thinks he's Bing Crosby."

Days earlier, we had made a preliminary survey of the locales and people we would need for our Venetian shoot. We needed a gondolier who could sing. I had auditioned dozens, and picked Papa. Now the losers were getting even by making fun of him. There was nothing I could do about it. Papa wouldn't sing. After all, he had to live with those guys after we were gone.

"Okay! Okay! Tell the son of a bitch to just move his lips. Make believe he's singing. We'll lay in the sound track back home."

That's why when my colleagues back in the States viewed the rushes in the projection room at the laboratory, they were treated to the sight of a typical Venetian gondolier intermittently moving his lips in silent pantomime, with my offstage voice on the sound track screaming, "Move your lips, you dumb bastard! *Canta! Canta!* Move your goddam lips, or I'll kill you!"

Yes, shooting on foreign locations is stimulating.

seven

Oh, Danny Boy

I was shooting an *I Spy* episode in a square next to the medina, in the Moroccan city of Marrakesh. The square was called "Place of the Dead" because, until well into the twentieth century, it was the place of executions, and the heads of the victims were impaled on pikes surrounding the square. The "Place of the Dead" may well be the most colorful and exciting ten acres in the world.

At that time, 1965, the people of Marrakesh had neither television nor movies. Very few homes had electricity, so even radio was scarce. The people came to the "Place of the Dead" for their entertainment. There were snake charmers, magicians, acrobats, and jugglers. Blue People from the Atlas Mountains were banging with hooked drumsticks on camel skin drums. And there were storytellers. All of the performers were surrounded by audiences sitting cross-legged and occasionally throwing a small coin into the entertainers' baskets. The storytellers drew the biggest audiences by far. As I wandered around the square, mentally choosing the sights that I wanted to capture on film, I stopped to watch the storytellers.

I watched these descendants of the medieval minstrels, weaving their tales of love and hate, adventure and romance; manipulating their wide-eyed audience with word, gesture, intonation, and grimaces. For those of us who aspire to be storytellers, I thought, this is the embodiment of our craft. If his father had not emigrated to America, Danny Thomas might have been standing there.

Danny was the ultimate raconteur. He didn't have an elaborate comic persona like Jack Benny, nor a machine gun

101

delivery like Bob Hope. He didn't put on lady's dresses like Berle or spout a stream of one-liners like Youngman. He told stories. He philosophized about the insanities of life. He talked about the idiosyncrasies of modern medicine, and about the spending habits of his daughter, Marlo, "Miss Charge Account of the Year."

Danny, born Amos Jacobs, was brought up in a tough neighborhood of Toledo, Ohio. "The kids on my block never played spin the bottle," he said. "They played spin the policeman." He was a high school dropout, and this was a great shame, because I never knew anyone with a greater capacity for absorbing and using knowledge than he.

For years, he had kicked around in second-rate night clubs and local radio. Shortly after he married Rosemarie, his career seemed to reach a dead end. One day, broke and despondent, he found himself in front of a church. Danny, a deeply religious man, entered the church to seek guidance and help in prayer. He knelt before a shrine to St. Jude, patron saint of the hopeless, and promised that if his career could be turned around, he would some day build a shrine to honor the saint.

Shortly after that low point, Danny got himself booked into the Fifty-One Hundred Club in Chicago. Maybe his skills as a performer had matured, maybe his timing was right, or maybe St. Jude had something to do with it. For whatever reason, he was a smash, and the magnificent St. Jude Memorial Hospital for Catastrophic Diseases in Children, in Memphis, Tennessee, was ultimately the fulfill-ment of his promise to the saint.

Word spread around the city of Chicago about the hook-nosed comic at the Fifty-One Hundred Club, who told an hilarious story about a man trudging down a dark and lonely road in search of a garage, from which he can borrow a jack with which to change a flat tire. "So suppose the guy wants to charge me to borrow the jack," he soliloquizes.

"How much can it be to borrow a ten-dollar jack for maybe a half hour?.... Maybe a dollar....Big deal!... If he needs it so bad, he can have his lousy dollar.... But he knows I'm in trouble....Where else can I get a jack at three o'clock in the morning?...He's got me over a barrel....He can charge whatever he wants....Two dollars.....Maybe three....Three dollars rent for a lousy ten dollar jack?.....Who says he has to stop at three dollars? Maybe five, six...."

By this time he has reached the garage, and he bursts in on the startled proprietor, screaming, "You can take your lousy jack and stuff it....!"

After the Fifty-One Hundred Club, Danny's career took off like a rocket. His fame spread from Chicago to New York, where he was booked into the fashionable Club Martinique. There is nothing so destructive to a comic's act as ad-libs from the audience, and the gang of comics from Lindy's were waiting for the Chicago phenomenon. Fat Jack Leonard, Phil Foster, Phil Silvers, and their cohorts were ganging up to clobber the intruding wonder boy on his opening night. Danny had been warned that the local comics were out to get him, but Milton Berle, the leading night club comic of his day, was also aware of their threat to Danny. Having met Danny in Chicago and liked him, he appointed himself Danny's defender.

Danny could not have had a more stalwart champion. Anyone who chose to cross words with Milton was doomed from the start. Milton's filing cabinet mind was loaded with comic material that he had shamelessly stolen from anybody and everybody. As he himself said, "Once, while watching Joey Bishop's act, I laughed so hard I nearly dropped my pencil and paper." Milton had a bottomless store of ripostes and crushers.

On the night of Danny's opening, Milton was seated at a table front and center. Midway through Danny's act, the heckling started and Milton rose to the challenge. In response to, "Did they think those jokes were funny in Chicago?" from the back of the house, Milton roared, "Don't pay any attention to him, Danny. He's suffering from tight underwear."

From the back of the house, "Hey, Milton. Who did you steal that from?"

From Milton, "Oh ho! He wants a battle of wits. I'll check half of mine so we can start even."

You will have gathered that Milton had not lifted his material from G.B. Shaw or Oscar Wilde, but whatever the source he had a lot of it. Under his barrage, the outgunned hecklers soon subsided. Danny went on to a highly successful engagement and a rapidly blossoming career. Until December 7, 1941.

By then Abe Lastfogel had taken over personal management of Danny's career. He told Danny that, until after the war, he was finished as a night club performer. He didn't ask him. He told him. When the war broke out, Abe was made head of the USO, the organization that put together entertainment packages for the troops, and throughout the war years, the USO was Danny's only employer.

After the war, Danny was reluctant to return to the night club grind. He was a family man, and working night clubs meant long stretches on the road, living in hotels. He made some pretty good theatrical films, but his work in pictures was intermittent at best. He wanted something more regular that would allow him to stay home. Television seemed to be the answer, and Abe Lastfogel was just the guy to arrange it. That leads us to the table on Stage Five of the Desilu lot on Cahuenga Boulevard.

With a commitment for a television season, Danny settled into a domestic routine. He applied for membership in the Hillcrest Country Club., where he had been a guest many times over the years when it was limited to Jewish membership and he was not eligible. After that restriction was lifted and non-Jews were welcome, Danny applied, and was turned down. He was understandably shocked.

He complained to the head of the membership committee: "I can't understand it. All the while that you were a restricted club, I ate here, I played golf and gin rummy here, I was a guest. Now that you've opened up the memberships for gentiles I apply and you turn me down. Why?"

"Because," he was told, "we decided that if we were going to admit gentiles they should look like gentiles."

According to Greek mythology, Hercules was required to perform twelve labors, each considered impossible to accomplish. He was ordered to clean the Augean stables, where, for countless years, three thousand oxen had been doing what oxen do. He had to kill a lion that was immune to mortal arrows. He had to conquer dragons and wild bulls. He had to perform the impossible, time after time. Big deal! In my first venture as a producer, I had to deliver a funny show about a crippled widower. Move over, Herc!

I became the producer of *The Danny Thomas Show* when Lou Edelman, who had preceded me, decided to concentrate on his *Wyatt Earp* show. Lou said that, after three years, he had scraped the bottom of the barrel for story premises.

In the hiatus preceding my first season as a producer, I called together my principal writing teams, Jack Elinson and Chuck Stewart, Mac Benoff, Shelley Keller, and Artie Stander. Danny was playing a date at the Sands Hotel in Las Vegas. I took my writers there, with their wives or whatever, as guests of the company. I had to get as many script assignments as possible out of the way before production started, because once we were in production most of my time would be spent on the stage.

Once a series is underway, a TV producer's principal responsibility is script preparation. Casting is minimal from week to week, because the series regulars carry most of the load. There is little or no new set construction. Cost control is automatically handled by computers. The scripts are the never-ending problem. It behooved me to get as much of the office work out of the way as possible in the between-season hiatus.

Right after breakfast in Las Vegas, we would gather around the pool, smear on the suntan oil, and pitch story ideas at one another.

This routine was not as self-indulgent as it may seem at first glance. When you're involved with a long-running show, you spend more time with your fellow-workers than you do with your family. If you don't get along well together, if you don't like one another, the whole structure is in trouble. Over a period of years, a minor irritation can become a bleeding wound. I firmly believed that it was good executive procedure to keep the people I worked with happy. With the cooperation of all concerned, we did our best to make the environment in which we spent endless days a pleasant one. At the studio there was always fresh coffee bubbling on the prop room stove, and donuts on the table. There was cold milk and ice cream in the refrigerator for the kids. Friends of the cast members were welcome visitors.

In Vegas, with cold drinks ever at hand, and between refreshing dips in the nearby pool, we would pitch and pitch, until we had accumulated from fifteen to twenty premises with which to start our thirty-nine episode season. The writers didn't know which of the accumulating story ideas would be assigned to them for further development, so every one unselfishly contributed embellishments to all of the premises.

At the end of a week of premise invention, I might say, "Mac, you take the Little Green Men premise and the Tooth Fairy one. Jack and Chuck, you do the Uncle Toonoose and the Rusty's Report Card stories. Shelley...." With all the stories assigned, the principal problem that faces weekly production was on the way to being solved. Or so you would think.

I came back from Vegas with a nice bundle of story assignments, most of them dealing with family situations, with which to start my first season as a producer-director. I was very proud of what had been accomplished, and everybody knows what comes after pride — a fall, right? My first day back, I learned that I had lost one of the principal members of the family. Jean Hagen, who had played Danny's wife in the series, decided that television was going nowhere, and she wanted out. She refused to sign up for the oncoming season. She was going back to features.

We couldn't just replace her. The viewers regarded the Danny Williams family very possessively. After all, they had been visiting that family regularly for the past three seasons. It wasn't acceptable simply to recast the part of the wife and mother of the Williams family and proceed as if nothing had happened. We would recast eventually, but first there had to be a transition period.

In passing, it's worth observing that the strong personal attachment that develops between the cast of a series and the audience gives the leading cast members tremendous negotiating power. They quickly become irreplaceable, and their salaries balloon up into the stratosphere.

I decided that the only thing to do about the Jean Hagen situation was to kill her.

Our writers were instructed to take the position that the unfortunate lady had suffered an untimely demise, in an unspecified manner, during the summer hiatus. The dialogue to dispose of her was to go like this: "Well, kids," Danny would say to his young son and daughter, "We've got to stick together closer than ever, now that Mom is gone. I know that she's up there watching over us, and that's what she would want."

Okay. Throw a shovelful of dirt on the coffin, and let's get on with the jokes.

The writers quickly wrote Jean out of the scripts they had already prepared and it seemed that we were back on track, but Fate wasn't through with us yet.

In the backyard of his Beverly Hills home, Danny was shooting baskets with his son, Tony, and you know how it is — Old Dad can't let his son out-shoot him or out-jump him. After all, it was practically yesterday that Old Dad was changing the young squirt's diapers. Old Dad will show him that he can still go up after the ball.

Danny didn't just break his ankle. He shattered it.

"At least two months in a wheelchair," said Dr. Danny Leventhal. The start of production was ten days away!

Call the writers back. Let's redesign the show. It'll be a funny show about a crippled widower.

We started the season with Danny Williams, recently widowed, in a wheelchair. He described the gruesome fate that would befall any kid who ever again left his or her skates at the head of the stairs for parents to trip over and break ankles. Then he gave them the Mom's-up-in-Heaven-watching-over-us speech. Then on with the funny stuff.

We were in the Top Ten, third or fourth, all season long.

Rating success in television is a self-perpetuating phenomenon. When you've got a hit show, all sorts of benefits accrue. Guest stars are readily available. Financing is practically thrust upon you. Choice time spots open up for your product. The success of *The Danny Thomas Show* brought many such benefits. Abe Lastfogel called me into his office to tell me that the Morris office had just signed a new client who was interested in getting into television, and he was giving me first crack at him. His name was Andy Griffith. Did I know about him? Yes, I did. He had broken into prominence with a hillbilly type of comedy record called

What It Was Was Football, and he was currently starring on Broadway in the title role of the musical, *Destry.* Did I have any ideas that might fit him? Give me a day or two.

Non-professionals have the mistaken idea that "ideas" are the foundation for television success. Not true. Ideas grow on every tree. Personalities are what count. Name a personality and any writer can pitch a dozen "ideas" that would work for him or her. Lucy? Sure. She's a sales girl in a big department store with a heart of gold and a head of ivory. Or you could have a lot of fun with her as a hotel telephone operator who keeps sticking her nose into the guests' affairs. How about she's the zany wife of an orchestra leader with a yen for show business? Oh, you like that one. Roseanne Barr? Okay. She's the sloppy, fat owner of a gay night club. Or, she's a sloppy, fat judge who throws zingers at the hookers and pushers who appear before her in night court. Wait a minute! Let's go in a different direction. She's the sloppy, fat wife in a sloppy fat household. The public will love it! It makes them feel superior.

Artie Stander and I came up with a formula for Andy Griffith. We knew that he had to be set in a rural environment, and we knew that his comedic strength lay in his talent for reacting. He had to be surrounded by funny characters and have some kind of home life. So we supplied him with an orphaned son and a motherly aunt.

Anyone could take it from there.

I was always greedy for scripts with which to feed the insatiable appetite of our weekly series. I concocted a plan to present Andy Taylor (that was the clever name we devised for Andy Griffith in the pilot) in a regular episode of *The Danny Thomas Show.*

The plot has Danny driving south to fill a club date in Miami. He is picked up for speeding by a country sheriff in the town of Mayberry. Danny quarrels with the sheriff, and winds up in jail. During the rest of the half-hour episode, we meet the sheriff's five-year-old son, his Aunt Bee, and a sampling of the town characters. The episode would serve as a pilot, and it wouldn't cost us a dime! I didn't know I was inventing the spinoff.

I went to New York to meet with Andy and his manager, Dick Linke, to try the idea out on them. They weren't enchanted with having to forgo a regular pilot, but they liked the format I proposed. As I found out later, Andy kinda figgered I was being straight with him. We shook hands on a deal.

I wanted five-year-old Ronnie Howard to play Andy's son. I had seen him in a failed pilot he had made with Bert Lahr, and I was not about to let him get away from me. His father, Rance Howard, had misgivings. He had been coerced into letting Ronnie do the Bert Lahr pilot, and he had lost sleep over it. He was genuinely concerned, because he didn't want little Ronnie to lose his childhood. I told him how we had protected the two children who worked on *The Danny Thomas Show*. They enjoyed coming to the studio. They bicycled and skated around the lot. Licensed teachers held them to the curriculum standards of the finest private schools. Rance Howard agreed to take a chance.

I never thought of anyone but Frances Bavier to play motherly Aunt Bee.

I persuaded Aaron Ruben, who had written and directed for *The Phil Silvers Show* (*Sergeant Bilko*), to leave his comfortable suburban home in Westchester and take over the producer's responsibilities.

During his Easter Week layoff from *Destry* Andy flew to California to do the spinoff. On the first day of preparation, he joined Danny, Artie Stander, and me around the reading table. That first day was nearly the last.

Our around-the-table readings were not for the faint-hearted. They usually sounded more like a barroom brawl than a rehearsal. Danny would express his disapproval of a line or a situation with sounds like those of a wounded bull moose. Artie, offended by such criticism of his writing, would respond with screams of outrage. As moderator of the session, I would have to top them with bellows for order. At the end of a typically raucous first day, Dick Linke came to me and said Andy would like a few words.

"Ahm sorry," Andy told me, "but Ah don't think this is for me. Ah cain't scream and yell like you fellers, so if that's the way it's gotta be, maybe Ah should just stick with what Ah know how to do and forget about this television thing."

Everything hung in the balance for the next two hours, while I labored to convince Andy that every show was different, that it took its character from the personality of the star. If he wanted a nice, quiet show, that's what he'd get. Finally, reluctantly, he agreed to give it a try.

Andy Griffith is not a funny man in the way that Jimmy Durante, or Red Skelton, or any of the clowns is funny. There is nothing of the baggy-pants comic about him. He is solid, substantial, and sane. He is also a very fine actor. None of these qualities has immediate comic value, but they create comedy when they are juxtaposed with zaniness, strangeness, and eccentricity. In less pretentious language, a sane man in a crazy world is funny.

I sought far-out characters for Andy's supporting cast, and I came up with Don Knotts to play Deputy Barney Fife, Jim Nabors to play Gomer Pyle, George Lindsey as Goober, Howard McNear as Floyd the barber, and Hal Smith as the town drunk, along with other assorted kooks. It was the finest collection of *meshugganahs* in television.

Writing for this wildly-varied cast was a challenge. Because each character was carefully designed, it was essential that integrity be maintained. Don Knotts' Barney Fife always had to be irascible, vain, swaggering, and boastful. Gomer Pyle a likeable goon, a cheerful simpleton, well-meaning but clumsy. The town barber, the town drunk, the gas station attendant — all had their inviolable characteristics.

This required a high quality of writing and since the baleful legacy of Senator Joseph (Tail Gunner Joe) McCarthy was still in evidence, many of the writers I wanted to use were blacklisted. Television was singularly vulnerable to the blacklist. Sponsors didn't care who bought their products. Right wing, left wing, or center, it was all the same to American Tobacco and Procter & Gamble. They didn't want anybody to be mad at them, so when Tail Gunner Joe pointed a finger at this or that writer, director, or actor, it was off with another head.

In upstate New York, the president of a chain of supermarkets, the Johnson Group, had signs printed reading "The makers of this product employ communists," which he posted on the shelves over the contaminated merchandise. Corporate executives panicked at the thought of having their products thus labeled.

West Coast television had a procedure for determining just how pure any member of the creative community was. Two weeks before the start of production, a list of credits for each episode of a series had to be submitted to the sponsor, the ad agency, and the network. The list of credits was forwarded to one of two prominent Hollywood actors — accepted by sponsors and networks as simon-pure — Adolphe Menjou, who was a little to the right of the Ku Klux Klan, or Ward Bond, slightly to the right of Menjou.

They, sitting with a copy of *Red Channels* close at hand, determined the virtue of the people on the credits list. God forbid that you had ever been seen reading a copy of *The Daily Worker*. If you were a member of any liberal organization, such as the Hollywood Independent Citizens Committee or the Theater Arts Club, you were a dead pigeon. If you had been named by any of the craven witnesses testifying before the House Committee on

UnAmerican Activities, it was time for you to look for a job outside of show business. Since writers are likely to be rebellious freethinkers by nature, a great many of them had earned Mr. Bond's or Mr. Menjou's disapproval.

Whenever I got a memo indicating that one of the names I had submitted was "not acceptable," my blood pressure shot up. It was hard enough to maintain a steady stream of scripts for two shows without the obstacles created by the Senator. Both my shows were doing well, and since sponsors and networks are notoriously reluctant to make waves, I was reasonably sure that, unless I was unreasonably blatant, they would look the other way while I took steps to solve my writing problems.

If Messers Menjou and Bond wouldn't clear a writer under his real name, there were any number of innocuous names in the phone book that they might like. Until the McCarthy era slid into well-deserved oblivion, many telephone subscribers in the Greater Los Angeles area would have been surprised to learn how important they were to my shows.

One way or another, under Aaron Ruben's skillful guidance, *The Andy Griffith Show* enjoyed a level of high quality, low-key, comedy writing that has seldom been duplicated. Regard a sample of that kind of writing. Andy and Barney are sitting on the front porch:

BARNEY
Did I ever tell you how I went overboard with
Thelma Lou on her last birthday?

ANDY
Did you get her something nice?

BARNEY

Nicest present I ever gave her. Know what I did?
Took her out to dinner.

ANDY

Took her out to dinner?

BARNEY

Well, yeah, you know. We usually go dutch.
Took her to Morelli's.

ANDY

No kidding. Morelli's?

BARNEY

Now there's a place to take a girl. Out on the
highway like that. Nice and secluded. Red check-
ered tablecloths.

ANDY

Fancy, fancy.

BARNEY

You know, they'll let you take a bottle in there.

ANDY

You don't drink though.

BARNEY

Nooo, haha.

ANDY

What'd you have to eat?

BARNEY

The DeLuxe Special. You know, you can hold it
down to a dollar eighty-five out there if you
don't have the shrimp cocktail.

ANDY

Did you have the shrimp cocktail?

BARNEY

Well, no. I told Thel let's not fill up. Minestrone
was delicious though.

ANDY

Oh, yeah. When that's made right it's really
something.

BARNEY

And for the main dish, Pounded Steak A La
Morelli.

ANDY

Oh?

BARNEY

It's really pounded, too. No question about it.
They got one of these open kitchens and you can
look right in there and see them pound it right
with your own eyes.

ANDY

Oh, yeah. Kinda see what you're getting.

BARNEY

I tell you, Andy, when that meal was finished I
did something I rarely do. I sent my compli-
ments back to the chef. They appreciate them

things. He kinda looked up from his pounding
and sort of waved at me.

ANDY

I'm gonna have to take Helen over there one of
these days.

BARNEY

Oh, she'd love it. Love it! It's not only the food
either. It's the atmosphere. They have the can-
dles on the table and the music, They got a
gypsy violinist out there. He must have played
six or eight songs standing over our table. Of
course, you gotta slip him a quarter.

ANDY

Yeah. Those fellers work on tips.

BARNEY

One thing about gypsies though. They're moody.

I love that kind of writing. It was done by a blacklisted
writer, bearing a name selected from page 326 of the Los
Angeles phone book.

eight

Alan Brady and Beyond

I had two shows solidly planted in the Top Ten. Both were sponsored by General Foods, which was represented by the Benton and Bowles advertising agency. Lee Rich was the head of their television department. Benton and Bowles also represented Procter & Gamble, and the head of advertising for that firm, "Havvy" Halverstadt, wanted to know why Lee Rich hadn't found some nice Top Ten shows for him.

Over a lunch at the Brown Derby, Lee told me that Procter & Gamble were willing to finance my next pilot project in return for first refusal. He wanted to know if I had a project in mind. I did.

Some time earlier, Harry Kalsheim, a fatherly, sixtyish gentlemen from the New York office of the William Morris Agency, had brought Carl Reiner to meet me. Carl told me that he had recently made a pilot of a premise that he had created for himself. Called *Head of the Family*, it was about the professional and domestic life of a writer for a TV comic. Carl and Barbara Britton had played the leads. It failed, and Carl figured he must have done something wrong. He wanted to hang around our successful operation for a while to see what he could learn. That was okay with me, but I wanted to see why his pilot hadn't made it. Carl was a talented writer and actor. It should have been a fine pilot.

The Morris office got me a print, and before I had screened five minutes of it I knew why it hadn't sold. Carl was all wrong for the part that he had written for himself. This was too bad, because the writing in the failed pilot was excellent. When I complimented Carl on the quality of his

117

writing, he told me that he had twelve more scripts that he had written during a summer spent on Fire Island in the expectation that his pilot would sell. Would I like to read them? I would. I did. I loved them.

I told Carl that I would like to take a crack at the material, if he would agree to let me recast it. Carl's professionalism was stronger than his ego. He said, "Sure. Have you got someone in mind?"

I said, "Yeah. A kid named Dick Van Dyke."

Before bringing Carl to me, Harry had touted me on to another "loser." He had insisted that Dick Van Dyke, the young leading man in the Broadway musical *Bye Bye Birdie*, should be on television. Apparently many other people had the same opinion, because Van Dyke had been cast as the lead in four separate pilot ventures. None of them had sold.

Yielding to Kalsheim's insistence, I had gone to see *Bye Bye Birdie*, and had concluded that Kalsheim was right: Van Dyke belonged on television. His jaw was a little too long, his rawboned body a little too angular, his walk a little too gangly. All of this made him, in my opinion, just right for television, which had shown a marked distaste for glamour boys who didn't fit comfortably into nonglamorous American living rooms.

After seeing *Bye Bye Birdie*, I had gone backstage and introduced myself to Van Dyke. I told him that sooner or later he'd hear from me. It turned out to be sooner.

I dug up two of Van Dyke's failed pilots. It was obvious to me that he had been miscast. He seemed uncomfortable with the characters he had been called on to portray. In both cases he had been cast as a wacky, dim-witted clown. Dick bears a startling resemblance to Stan Laurel, of the immortal team of Laurel and Hardy. This led to the conclusion that he should play the kind of parts Stan Laurel played. As a matter of fact, Dick can do a marvelous impersonation of Laurel. He can walk like him and he can even pop out his lower lip and look amazingly like him. But he isn't Stan Laurel. He's Dick Van Dyke, a nice looking, sturdy, sane, boy-next-door type. In my opinion, that was the best way to present him on TV.

At this point, by recalling how easily I spotted the mistakes my peers had made, I must sound like a pretentious know-it-all. I apologize, but the fact is that sometimes I'm right and they're wrong, and quite frequently it's the other way around.

I asked Carl to go back east to see Van Dyke. After attending his performance, Carl phoned to tell me that he agreed that Dick would be perfect as his alter ego. From that moment on, the project was green lighted.

I told Lee Rich that I was prepared to take Procter & Gamble up on their offer to finance any pilot I chose to do in return for first refusal. I asked the Morris office to draw up the contracts, but Abe Lastfogel wasn't happy. During a lengthy luncheon at the Hillcrest Country Club, he persuaded me to ditch Procter & Gamble and let Danny Thomas provide the financing. He argued that giving first refusal to Proctor and Gamble seriously handicapped the project, because if they turned it down, nobody else would touch it. In other words, their first refusal added up to last refusal. Furthermore, giving them first refusal deprived us of the considerable advantage of putting it up for competitive bidding among potential sponsors.

Who was I to argue with Abe Lastfogel, the head of the largest talent agency in the entertainment world? I accepted Danny's financing and Danny accepted a hunk of ownership in *The Dick Van Dyke Show*.

My newly acquired partner was responsible for a major casting accomplishment. To play Laura Petrie, Dick's wife, Carl and I had been interviewing young leading ladies by the bushel. We had even gone to New York to examine the talent market there. We weren't happy with the results.

In a casual conversation with Danny, we voiced our frustration.

"How about that kid with three names?" he asked.

What the hell did that mean, "kid with three names"?

"You know, when we were looking for someone to replace Sherry Jackson in my show, she auditioned. She was the best, but she didn't look as if she belonged in my family. Her nose went the wrong way. So we had to pass on her, but she was great."

I remembered her. She was very good. Yeah, she had three names — Mary something something. What else did I remember about her? Among her credits, she had played "Happy Hotpoint," dancing on top of kitchen appliances, and she had been the telephone operator on *Richard Diamond, Private Detective*, but they never showed anything but her legs. Nice legs.

Our casting director tracked down the girl with three names, Mary Tyler Moore. She was hard to find, because her career had been languishing for the past several years. She was semi-retired from show business.

She was glad to be a part of *The Dick Van Dyke Show*, but she didn't expect too much from it. Her luck hadn't been good lately. Maybe she could come out of it with enough money for new carpets and drapes.

The rest of the casting was a breeze. I had been a fan of Rose Marie since she was Baby Rose Marie, a precocious five-year-old belting out songs from the stage of the Brooklyn Paramount Theatre. She had developed into a fine comedienne, with excellent timing and a sharp delivery. She was glad to come aboard; and as soon as she was set, she started making a pitch for her buddy, Morey Amsterdam. Morey was exactly what we needed to complete the writing team featured in the show, the writers for the fictional *Alan Brady Show*.

From the beginning it was apparent that we had a remarkable chemistry working for us. Dick, Mary, Morey, Rose Marie, and Richard Deacon blended together miraculously, so that there was little need for guidance. To this day, Dick likes to tell how masterfully I molded his performance by calling him aside after a rehearsal. He waited patiently for directorial instruction. I hemmed for a moment and then said, "Dick, make your voice go up and down more." Period. Actually, I always directed all their performances with a light hand. If it ain't broke, don't fix it.

I shot the pilot on Stage 5 of the Cahuenga Studio in April of 1961. I did it three-camera style, because I felt that the kind of comedy we were presenting needed an audience presence to give it a boost. The shoot went very well, and by the time I had edited the show, dubbed it, scored it, and attached the main titles, I was sure we had a winner.

The finished print was due out of the laboratory on a Monday morning, a couple of weeks after I shot the show. I arranged to pick it up at eleven o'clock, in time to make a noon plane to New York, where I was scheduled to screen it for a battery of prospective buyers. I showed up at the delivery door of the laboratory on time, and said to the man at the desk, "I'm here for the print of the *Van Dyke Show.*"

"What are you talking about?" the man wanted to know. "A guy picked that up as soon as we opened at eight o'clock."

"What guy?" I demanded.

"Here. He signed the book."

The name in the book was George Giroux, Procter & Gamble's man in charge of West Coast television production. By the time I got to New York, late in the afternoon, Procter & Gamble had not only screened the pirated print, they had placed an order for the series.

They had gotten the first refusal they wanted, and it hadn't cost them a penny.

Jim Aubrey, the president of CBS, didn't enjoy being pushed around by Procter & Gamble, but since their daytime business — the "soaps" — was the difference between profit and loss for the network, he had to shut up and take it. He didn't want *The Dick Van Dyke Show* on his network, because it had a show business background and, in his book, that made it a loser. He asked me, almost plaintively, if I couldn't make Van Dyke a real estate salesman instead of a TV comedy writer.

"Sorry," I said.

With Procter & Gamble backing me up, I could stand tough.

Aubrey put us on Tuesday night at eight, which meant seven in the midwest, a lousy time spot for an adult comedy.

We went on the air in October of 1961. We didn't do too well. Something was wrong with the show. More specifically, something was wrong with Van Dyke. He didn't seem at ease with the dialogue. It took us a good part of the first season to identify the problem; then it took more time to correct it. Dick's substandard performance, combined with the poor time spot, made it not surprising that we had disappointing ratings. Toward the end of March, we were told that we were canceled.

I called Lee Rich and implored him to get me an appointment with the head of advertising for Procter & Gamble.

"I can't let them kill this show. We've got our problems licked. The show is going to be great," I insisted.

Reluctantly, Lee got me an appointment with Havvy Halverstadt, in Procter & Gamble's home city, Cincinnati. He would see me at ten o'clock on the following Monday.

On the Sunday night preceding my appointment, Lee was my guest at a black-tie Directors Guild awards dinner. He had agreed to come into the lion's den with me. Right from the dinner table, still in black tie, we taxied to the airport to catch the twelve o'clock Redeye Express. The next morning, haggard and owl-eyed, we gulped coffee from room service and grabbed a quick shower.

"How about it, Lee?" I asked. "Are you going to back me up when I make my pitch to Havvy?"

"I don't know." he told me.

"What does that mean? You're their media adviser. After I make my pitch, Havvy is going to turn to you and ask, 'What does Benton and Bowles think about this?' Are you going to say 'I don't know?'"

"Maybe. I don't know what I'm going to say, until I hear what you're going to say."

Havvy Halverstadt was a Lincolnesque figure, tall and stately. He exuded dignity and power, which was not surprising since he controlled the spending of several hundreds of millions with the media. Awesome.

He ushered us into the conference room next to his office. After the conventional preliminaries, I took over. I did everything but get down on one knee and sing "Mammy."

"You can't drop the show," I told him. "You'll regret it forever. We had some trouble with Dick's character, but we've got it fixed. Van Dyke is going to be great. The problems he had were our fault. From now on, he's going to win us a closetful of Emmys. The trouble was that we had him speaking dialogue written by a Bronx Jew, to be spoken by that Bronx Jew. It sounded all wrong coming out of the mouth of an Indiana Baptist. We fixed it. Now we know how to put a pair of balls on Van Dyke...."

"Excuse me," Havvy said. He rose from his chair, and stalked to the door.

"Oh, shit!" I said to myself. "Me and my foul mouth! I blew it! I've lost him."

Havvy closed the door to the adjoining room, came back to his chair and sat down.

"There's an unmarried secretary in that room," he told me. "Now, just how are you going to put a pair of balls on Van Dyke?" A half hour later he rescinded the cancellation, and took us to lunch.

I got a hero's reception when I returned to the studio. The cast had been buried in gloom since they had learned of the cancellation. In one brief season, everybody connected with the show had blended into a happy, loving family. The reprieve incited a celebration. Carl and Dick strung a "Welcome Home, Conquering Hero" banner over the door to my office. The prop man broke out a case of champagne. But our joy was short-lived.

Havvy came out of the spell I had cast upon him, and regretted his impulsive decision to renew his sponsorship of the *Van Dyke Show*. He decided that he only wanted half of it. He would sponsor the show on alternate weeks, which left the other half of the show unsold.

Jim Aubrey had been furious at Havvy's decision to renew the show, but now that half of it remained unsponsored, he warned me that he wouldn't keep a time spot open for anything less than a fully-sponsored show.

Back to New York. Sol Leon, of the Morris office, lined up appointments with potential sponsors for me. I struck gold on the first try. The media chief for the Lorillard Tobacco Company loved Mary's legs. He said, "Another reason I like the show is that Laura and Rob Petrie are the first married couple on television who look like they have any fun in bed."

I was able to present a fully-sponsored show to Jim Aubrey. He wasn't happy.

In October of 1962, the show went on the air in a new time spot. For the next four years *The Dick Van Dyke Show* was a fixture in the Top Ten. It received sixty-four Emmy nominations, carried away twenty-one Emmy awards, three Golden Globes, and countless other commendations. More importantly, when it went off the air after a hundred fifty-eight episodes, it left behind a storehouse of precious memories.

Among them is my memory of a snatch of dialogue. Five-year-old Ritchie, seated at the dinner table with his parents, drops a bomb.

> RITCHIE
> Daddy, where did I come from?

> ROB
> [stammers and stutters]
> Well, Ritchie, when mommy and I decided we
> wanted a little boy to love, we...

> RITCHIE
> [interrupts]
> I was inside Mommy, wasn't I?

> ROB
> Oh... We didn't know you knew about....

> RITCHIE
> Everybody knows that.

> LAURA
> Ritchie, why did you ask where you came from
> if you know?

> RITCHIE
> Because I don't know.

> ROB
> But you just said you came from Mommy.

RITCHIE
Oh, I know that. I mean where did I come
from.....like Freddie came from Patterson, New
Jersey.

Then there was the show that Mary thought would be
her chance to escape from her job as a straight woman and
get to do some funny stuff herself. Carl had assured her that
an upcoming script, one of the best he had ever written, made
her the focus of an hilarious situation. Mary could hardly
wait for the script to come to the table. The day came when
the cast finally got a chance to read "Never Bathe on
Sunday." It was, indeed, a brilliantly funny script, with a
very clever gimmick. Mary was, as Carl had promised, the
focus of the plot, but she was offstage all the time! Her toe
was caught in the bathtub faucet. She was heard pleading,
complaining, and berating, but she was never seen.

Mary was crushed. She stormed away from the table
to lock herself in her dressing room, where she remained for
ten minutes. Then, like the professional she is, she stormed
back to the table to take up her job.

Carl was incomparable at coming up with comedy
premises with which everybody could identify. Not that
everybody knew someone who had caught their toe in a
bathtub faucet, but everyone knew somebody to whom that
sort of thing could happen. Many of Carl's premises were
culled from his personal experiences or from those of people
he knew. For instance, his neighbor gave him the idea for "A
Bird in the Head Hurts." Her son had been continually
assaulted by a blue jay intent on using the boy's hair for a
nest. The advice given to the distraught mother by an
S.P.C.A. official was "Let him wear a pith helmet."

"*Gezundheit*, Darling" was based on Carl's experience
with his allergies. A plague of sneezing attacks led him to
believe that he might be allergic to his wife, or his children,

or his neighbors. He was relieved to learn that a hidden cat was the cause of his affliction.

"Never Name a Duck" was the tale of Ritchie's attachment to a duckling which quickly outgrew its home in the Petrie's sink. It was based on Carl's experience with a duckling that his children had adopted. Carl's wife, Estelle, actually expressed her concern for the duckling's well-being, saying, "He looks pale."

"October Eve" was based on the experience of Bill Persky. At an art gallery, he had spotted a nude painting that bore a startling resemblance to his wife.

"That's My Boy" was based on an idea I pitched to Bill Persky and Sam Denoff. It was destined to have a remarkable effect on many careers. The story centered on Rob's suspicion that his newborn son may not be his but rather the result of a mixup in the hospital where the Petrie's baby and the son of Mr. and Mrs. Peters were born.

Because of the similarity in names, Laura Petrie and Mrs. Peters repeatedly received each other's gifts, flowers, and candy. That confusion, combined with Rob's conviction that the newborn babe resembles neither him nor Laura, leads him to conclude that each couple was given the other's baby. Rob makes an indignant phone call.

ROB

Hello, Mr. Peters? I think we have something of yours, and you have something of ours....A basket of dried figs?....Oh, yes. Those must be from my wife's Aunt Bertha. I didn't mean that. You know, Mr. Peters, there's a great similarity in our names...... Yes, I am one of the writers of the *Alan Brady Show*......Well, I'm glad you like it, but I want to get this thing settled. You know, Mr. Peters, both our wives gave birth to baby boys at the same time in the same hospital, and

the hospital was very busy.... What am I getting
at? Mr. Peters, may I ask you a personal question? Who does your baby look like?.....Well,
that's what I thought, because our baby doesn't
look like either of us either.....You're taking this
pretty lightly....Okay. We live right around the
block.....Oh, you know our address....Okay. I'll
expect you.

Some minutes later the doorbell rings and Rob opens
the front door.

> VOICE
> [Outside the door]
> Mr. Petrie? We're Mr. and Mrs. Peters.

> ROB
> Come in.

An attractive young black couple enter carrying a
basket of figs and smiling broadly. Rob stares at them, mouth
agape.

> MR. PETERS
> Would you like to swap some figs for some flow-
> ers?

> LAURA
> Won't you come in and sit down?

> MRS. PETERS
> Thank you. I'm still a little wobbly.

> LAURA
> Me, too. But not as wobbly as my husband.

MRS. PETERS
I know I shouldn't be up and around but I
wanted to be in on the fun.

LAURA
I understand.

ROB
[To Mr. Peters]
Why didn't you tell me on the phone?

MR. PETERS
And miss the expression on your face?

ROB
Yeah....Did I give you a good one?

MR. PETERS
A beaut!

ROB
I'm sorry. I haven't been myself lately. We've
just had a baby.....Oh, yeah. You did, too. How
about some coffee?

Laura starts to get up, but Rob pushes her down and
starts for the kitchen.

ROB
I'll make it, honey. Do you want to see the baby
we tried to pawn off on you?

He directs the Peters to the bassinet.

MR. PETERS
Hey, that's a beautiful baby...and he looks
exactly like you.

LAURA
Do you really think so?

MR. PETERS
No, but why start him off again?

They all LAUGH.
FADE OUT.

Following the established routine, we sent copies of
the script to the sponsors, the agency, and the network. The
first protest came from Procter & Gamble. Their representative, George Giroux, the print pirate, called me and said,
"We're afraid of that script. You're making fun of the fact
that the couple is black."

"No, George," I told him. "We're making fun of the
fact that Rob Petrie is a dope."

"This is 1963," George said. "There are riots in the
south. There's a big civil rights movement. We don't want to
offend anybody. We've got to be careful."

"I'll be careful, George."

"Well....Okay."

The next attack came from Lee Rich. He told me that
the Benton and Bowles agency had no intention of letting
their client, Procter & Gamble, risk their reputation by
approving "That's My Boy." He wasn't placated by the same
speech that had silenced George Giroux.

I said, "Tell you what I'll do. There will be three
hundred and fifty people in the audience when we shoot the
show. If any one of them finds it offensive, I will reshoot the

ending at my own expense. I'll give you a Chinese couple, or American Indian, or Eskimo. Whatever you want."

Rich accepted my offer.

I had a tougher time with the network. They were concerned about the episode's effect on the affiliated stations south of the Mason-Dixon Line. They reluctantly accepted the same assurance I had given Lee.

Greg Morris and Mimi Dillard were cast as Mr. and Mrs. Peters. When the handsome couple made their entrance, there was a moment of shocked silence, then the audience went crazy. It was the longest laugh in the whole five-year history of *The Dick Van Dyke Show* — so long that it had to be trimmed to fit the episode into its allotted air time.

After the telecast, the mail came in by the satchel full. It was congratulatory, laudatory, wholeheartedly approving. We had shown an attractive, cultured black couple going one up on their white counterpart.

I saved the mail. It was not the first time I had received mail on the subject of race. On *The Danny Thomas Show*, Amanda Randolph, a highly respected black character actress, had played the housekeeper for the Williams household. Whenever Danny or any member of his family showed physical affection for Amanda — a kiss on the cheek, an arm over the shoulder — I could count on a shower of hate mail.

"When I want to see a white man petting a gorilla, I'll go to the zoo."

"I don't allow niggers in my living room and you got no right to put them there."

One of the peculiarities of this kind of mail, aside from its crudeness, was that much of it was written in the same handwriting, and with the same postmark. The names were different. It was an obvious attempt by some sick people to make themselves seem like many more than they were.

Just as the earlier hate mail had been uniformly negative, the mail for "That's My Boy" was almost totally approving. Somewhere along the line, in the eight or nine years since the Amanda Randolph episodes, a change had occurred. I didn't know how or why, but I suspected it was related to the burgeoning civil rights movement.

Contracts for a TV series are usually written for a five-year period. Usually, at the end of that term, the owners of a successful show can negotiate an extension on a profitable basis, but the people connected with the *Van Dyke Show* had other ideas. Warmed by the success and approval that they had enjoyed for the past five years, they wanted to move on to other pastures. Rich picture offers were waiting for Dick and Mary. Carl wanted to try his hand at a screenplay. Although the sponsors were ready to make a greatly improved deal for an extension, our three key people would have none of it.

All I could do was tell them I loved them, and wish them good luck. While I was working on *The Van Dyke Show*, Aaron Ruben was busily tending the store over on the *Andy Griffith* stage. Early in that show's career, we had picked up a hunk of talent called Jim Nabors. Andy had heard Jim perform in an obscure Santa Monica night club, and had directed us to him. Jim had an extraordinary voice. It was of operatic quality, which was utterly inconsistent with his gangly, country boy appearance.

He was incorporated into *The Griffith Show* under Aaron's tutelage. Aaron built a character for him, which grew in popularity until it became obvious that the character could sustain a show of its own. That show became *Gomer Pyle, U.S.M.C.*

The armed forces offer several levels of "cooperation" to filmmakers. "Total cooperation" means technical advisers to guide them through the maze of military procedures, access to military installations, the unlimited use of uniforms, equipment, and personnel and, if needed, aircraft, naval vessels, and tanks. "Limited cooperation" means some of the above, at the discretion of the brass. "Non-cooperation" means "stay off our property."

The degree of cooperation depends on a judgment as to whether the picture or series concerned will be good for the image of the particular branch of our armed forces. Our series was designed to show how a bumbling but well-meaning country boy makes good as a Marine, because he possesses qualities of integrity, honor, and perseverance. The Marine Corps brass, ever on the lookout for a few good men, liked that. When I went to Washington to solicit cooperation, the Marine Corps told us we could have anything we wanted.

We were allowed to use the base at Camp Pendleton as our main set. If we needed guns, uniforms, or whatever, all we had to do was ask. If we wanted a squad, a platoon, or a brigade marching in the background, there they were.

The show added a term to the Marine Corps' vocabulary. A recruit with two left feet who couldn't keep out of trouble was called a "Gomer."

General Foods had bought television's first spinoff, *The Andy Griffith Show*, and they performed another first in the case of *Gomer Pyle, U.S.M.C.*. They bought it on no more than a description of the proposed format. It was a smart move for them. The show was an immediate success, and that created a unique situation. I had four shows on CBS — all of them in the Top Ten. Jim Aubrey, president of CBS, hadn't wanted any of them on his network. He considered *Andy Griffith* and *Gomer Pyle* "too shit-kicking" (too rural), *Danny Thomas* and *Dick Van Dyke* too "show biz."

According to Greek mythology, Sisyphus offended the gods and was condemned to roll a huge boulder up a steep hill through all eternity. When he got it to the top of the hill, the boulder rolled down to the bottom, so that he had to start over, again, and again, and again.

That's what doing a weekly television show is like. As soon as you've completed the task, you have to start over again. There's always the danger that it will become a routine, and when the excitement goes out of your work, you're in trouble.

I loved doing audience shows. The audience brought excitement into what could otherwise have become a tedious chore. Comedy shows have something extra going for them. The sound of hundreds of people laughing is a wonderful mood elevator. It produces a better high than anything that comes out of a bottle, and when you view the final results of your work in the screening room, there is a sense of accomplishment that must be like what a mountain climber feels when he reaches the top.

Why is everybody laughing? The break-up party at the end of the run of *The Dick Van Dyke Show* in 1966. To my left are Richard Deacon, little Larry Mathews and his mother, an unidentified lady, Ronnie Jacobs (Danny's nephew), Morey Amsterdam, Mary Tyler Moore, Dick Van Dyke, Bud Malone (the cutter), Rose Marie, Tony Guy, Carl Reiner, John Rich, a crew member, Earle Hagen, and another crew member.

A Television Academy dinner. Comedy was the subject, and from the left, the dais was made up of Joe Flynn, Carl Reiner, Groucho Marx, me, Bill Dana, and Tim Conway.

Directing Cosby and Culp in the Hong Kong pilot of *I Spy*. It's obviously okay for the director to catch pneumonia.

Bill Cosby's transportation is being led by two ladies whom we pressed into service. Holding Bill's foot is my wife, Frankie. Holding the camel's rope is Bill's mother.

On location in Hong Kong for the pilot of
I Spy in 1964. We were shooting in 16mm.

⌐ad Said and I look for a good place
to shoot an *I Spy* scene in Hong
Kong, 1965.

Leon Chooluck and I
scouting locations in
Russia, for *I Spy*, 1966.

Danny Arnold, William Windom, and I receiving these Emmys for *My World and Welcome to It* in 1970. They weren't enough to keep the show on the air.

Directing the eponymous star in the pilot of *The Don Rickles Show*, 1971.

Two gala events. With Marlo Thomas at one, with Mel
Blanc (left) and Phil Harris at the other.

A world-record fish I nabbed at my favorite fishing grounds in Baja California, 1984.

The afternoon before the Hall of Fame ceremony, I was introducing some of the folks from *The Andy Griffith Show* to an audience at Disney World. From left, Don Knotts, Aaron Rubin, Earle Hagen, Andy Griffith, and George Lindsey, 1992.

Being greeted by Mickey Mouse the night in 1992 when the six of us were inducted into the Televison Hall of Fame. Back row from left, Ted Koppel, Ted Turner, Bill Cosby. Front row from left, Andy Griffith, Dinah Shore, and me.

1994 finds our family still
going strong. My bride
of sixty-three years,
Frankie Leonard.

The proud father with son, Steven, and daughter, Andy.

In the decade of the sixties, I more or less specialized in directing pilots. I made them for T and L Productions, which was the partnership I had formed with Danny Thomas. I made them for other companies, in return for royalties or profit participation. Usually the star of the series got the biggest percentage, fifty per cent in the case of Andy Griffith, even more for Danny Thomas. The creator — Carl Reiner on *The Dick Van Dyke Show* — would get a piece, and there might be something for indispensable cast members, like Bill Cosby in *I Spy*. I would get what was left, which was usually in the area of thirty per cent, give or take a few points.

Thirty-five thousand dollars was a good price for a half-hour show. Our original prices were thirty thousand an episode for *The Danny Thomas Show*, thirty-five thousand for *Andy Griffith*, and forty thousand for *Dick Van Dyke*. Because *Van Dyke* was canceled after the first season, I was able to get forty-five thousand when they brought it back for the second season. All the shows had automatic yearly increases of ten percent.

The standard contract called for thirty-nine episodes a year, with thirteen repeats. You had to make your profit, if any, out of the first run. If your show was a hit, there was a good chance a network would buy it for "stripping" — that is, to play five repeat episodes a week in a non-prime-time spot.

The net from such figures, if applied to today's prices, would be astronomical. *Cheers* carries a weekly price tag of half a million. Further, nobody anticipated the rich rewards of syndication. In the sixties, *The Andy Griffith Show* sold to

Viacom for eight million. In the eighties, *The Bill Cosby Show*
sold for more than half a billion!

All the pilots I directed went on the air. Some of them
enjoyed a nice, long run, others vanished like smoke. *Lassie*
was one of the more durable ones. I directed the first six *Lassie*
shows; and in the process I learned how to direct lions,
alligators, bulls, and other assorted members of the animal
kingdom. The writers of the show had a continuing problem.
Lassie had to do something heroic every episode. Doing
something heroic usually involved overcoming a villainous
antagonist. It was easier to make an animal the antagonist
than a human; thus the proliferation of beasts. I will always
remember an episode I directed with lions.

The story line dealt with a lion that had escaped from
a circus. Somehow or other, the lion wound up in the kitchen
of Lassie's household. Lassie, fearless creature that she is,
intimidates the beast and keeps it at bay until it can be
recaptured by its trainer, thus saving young Tommy Rettig
from being eaten.

Mel Koontz supplied us with lions from his training
ranch in Thousand Oaks. When you undertake to make a
picture with lions, you quickly learn that you need an assortment of them, just as you need an assortment of collies to
make a Lassie film. Lassie has to have a stand-in, so she won't
be tired and surly from too much time under the lights. There
is a barking Lassie, a running, jumping, swimming Lassie,
and a beautiful, well-groomed Lassie, for close ups. You see,
there's specialization in the canine kingdom, too.

Some of the Lassies are male, some are female. Only
Rudd Weatherwax, the trainer, and the other Lassies know
the difference. In the matter of lions, Mel Koontz had friendly
lions, and nasty ones. He had lions for petting, and lions for
snarling and roaring. For instance, Rajah was a placid old
cow of a lion. When you wanted him to move over, you
kicked him into place. King was a real mean lion. When you

wanted him to move over, you said, "Please," and hoped he would oblige.

I had gotten to the kitchen scene, in which we had to use mean old King. He was required to burst into the kitchen and stalk about, snarling and baring his fangs — which he loved doing — while twelve-year-old Tommy Rettig cowered under the sink. Just in time, Lassie would come to the rescue.

We took every conceivable precaution to safeguard the twenty or more people who would be on the sound stage while the unpredictable King was working. We encircled the kitchen set with a ten-foot-high wall of chicken wire. Mel Koontz constructed a tunnel that guided King from his cage to the set, then stood by with an electric cattle prod and a pistol loaded with blanks.

When all was ready, the cameras rolled, and Koontz lifted the gate of King's cage. The ill-tempered beast came rushing down the chute, into the kitchen. Assessing the situation, he decided he didn't like the cast-iron stove. Whap! He took a swipe at it, and shattered it into a dozen pieces. That's right. A big black cast iron stove. Whap! Then, King looked around, roared a couple of times, and charged the chicken wire fence.

Chicken wire is undoubtedly fine for confining chickens, but it is not effective for restraining lions. King burst through the frail barrier as though it were tissue paper, disappearing into the forest of sets, props and furniture which clogged the stage.

People scattered in all directions. If there was something to climb, they climbed it. If there was something to hide behind, they hid.

The stage on which we were working was part of the lot that now houses TV station KTTV. Our unit manager had the sudden, frightening thought that someone might open the door that led to Sunset Boulevard, and we would have a bad lion loose. He screamed, "Somebody get to that door! Keep it closed!"

Nineteen-year-old Rudd Weatherwax Junior raced around the encumbrances, and arrived at the door just in time to meet King coming from the other direction. Junior froze. Mel Koontz came charging around the corner. Junior was statue-still. King was stalking around him, sniffing him, poking him with his muzzle.

"Stay that way! Don't move!" Koontz yelled. "He won't hurt you, if you don't move!" He approached King slowly, brandishing his cattle prod. King backed away. Koontz herded him into his cage, which was all that King had really wanted in the first place.

When the people had come down from high places, and emerged from behind prop boxes, everybody crowded around Junior to congratulate him on his heroism.

"Wow!" Tommy Rettig exclaimed. "How you stood there! You never moved when that big old lion went around and around you, sniffing and sniffing!"

"Yeah," Junior responded. "I've got to tell you, I surely gave him plenty to sniff at!"

I got into trouble with Walter Brennan when I directed the pilot and the early episodes of *The Real McCoys*. That title, by the way, is redundant. The term "McCoy" has come to mean "real," as in "it's the McCoy." That semantic breach didn't seem to damage the property, which ran forever. Walter Brennan, the star of the series, had a turkey farm up north, on the Pacific coast. He always had a few wrapped and dressed turkeys in the trunk of his car, just in case anyone wanted a turkey. If they didn't know they wanted a turkey, Walter would convince them.

A writer for *TV Guide* was on the set when I told the series producer, Irving Pincus, "If Walter would spend as much time learning his lines as he does selling those goddam turkeys, we could all go home early." The writer overheard me, and my careless remark appeared as a quote in his *TV Guide* story. The roof fell in on me.

Some friendly soul called the story to Walter's attention. He read it, retired to his dressing room in a huff, and didn't come out for the rest of the day. The incident cost the company several thousand dollars. I felt guilty. I was tempted to reimburse the company for its loss, but I overcame the temptation.

I apologized to Walter, but it didn't help much. Although I directed him in the first six episodes of the series, I never made much eye contact with Walter thereafter, even though I bought a twenty-pound turkey from him.

I directed the pilot and early episodes of a short-lived series called *Good Morning World*. The only memorable thing about it was an actress named Goldie Hawn. To give you some idea of how brilliantly she played her character, I had directed several episodes before I realized that I wasn't dealing with a lovable, flaky, dumb blonde, but with a lovable, intelligent, and talented actress.

When Lew Grade (later to become Sir Lew Grade, and still later, Lord Grade) came to America in 1969, he enlisted me to direct and produce a series to be made in England, starring a well-loved British comedienne, Millicent Martin. I put together a show about a couple of airline hostesses, who frolicked though many countries, offering "coffee, tea or me."

Since I made the series in England, British law and the British theatrical unions required that I use British actors and writers almost exclusively. *From a Bird's Eye View* had a limited run in America, largely because of its strongly British flavor. British humor doesn't seem to satisfy the American appetite. However, the series enjoyed many replays in England, and it did very well in the international market.

I had a good time working in England. I enjoyed the people, and Lew Grade supplied me with a car and driver, a generous expense allowance, and a charming apartment in Grosvenor House, overlooking Hyde Park. Consequently, when he called me a couple of years later to ask me to undertake a series starring Shirley MacLaine — who I admired greatly — I was happy to oblige.

It was a mistake.

Grade told me that Shirley had agreed to do a half-hour series for the ABC network, which had given Grade a full-season commitment. They were depending on me to come up with a premise. I met with Mel Shavelson, then president of the Writers Guild of America; we put together a formula that had Shirley as an investigative reporter, struggling with the responsibilities of a single parent when she wasn't globe-trotting in the exercise of her craft. The show was called *Shirley's World*.

I submitted the premise to Shirley during an afternoon meeting at her home in the San Fernando Valley. Shirley later described the meeting in her best-selling book, *You Can't Get There From Here*, in these terms:

"...his shirt was bright orange, matching an orange tie with black circles and an orange handkerchief that spilled over the edge of his jacket pocket. Sheldon slid his finger across his brow, moving the accumulated sweat to the left side, and flicked a spray of salt water into my garden."

That description does more credit to Shirley's imagination than it does to my taste in wardrobe. My wife would kill me if I wore a bright orange shirt. An orange tie with black circles? May heaven forgive Shirley. Countess Mara never will. And I don't sweat much!

Shirley accepted the premise I described, and I assigned Mel Shavelson to write the introductory script. As with the Millie Martin show, we were severely limited in the number of Americans we could use. Since that same show had made me painfully aware of the discrepancies between British and American tastes in humor, I engaged Frank Tarloff to rewrite and edit the British material, hoping thus to minimize culture shock. Frank had just won an Oscar for his widely-acclaimed script of *Father Goose*, starring Cary Grant and Leslie Caron.

The rules allowed me to have six scripts — out of the twenty-six needed to fill out the season — written by American writers. I called in some outstanding IOUs, to get the services of writers who had scored heavily for me on the *Thomas, Van Dyke* and *Griffith* shows. Carl Reiner, Jim Brooks, Garry Marshall, and a couple of other literary giants contributed. I thought we were in good shape with scripts.

It wasn't until we were actually in production and on the air that I found out Shirley didn't agree with me.

I had contracted to deliver a comedy to the ABC network, but it seemed that was not what Shirley had in mind. She didn't like the character that had been written for her. She wanted to play, quoting from her book, "...a girl who doesn't give too much of a crap the way fellows think." In her own words, she wanted to be "...a woman who knew what she wanted to do, and what she wanted to do would not be tied down to one boyfriend in London. She could have boyfriends all over the world, and if she wanted to go to bed with one of them every once-in-a-while, well, that would be all right, too."

I didn't disagree with her about the kind of character she wanted to play, but it wasn't what I had contracted to deliver, nor what the network was prepared to accept. Shirley was pulling in one direction, I in another. Between us, the series was torn apart.

I had to do a lot of transatlantic commuting to stay abreast of my ongoing American projects. When I was in America, I kept in touch with my British staff by an exchange of audio cassettes, via overnight mail. I could get more than an hour of monologue on the tape, so it was better than long distance phoning. I still have a cassette, sent by Ray Austin, the associate producer-director I had left in charge while I was out of England. In it, he says, "Well, she did it again. She sent word down from her dressing room that she wasn't going to do the shot until the scene was rewritten. Frank Tarloff went up to see what she wanted, and made some changes, but we still didn't get a shot until after the lunch break."

The series was a mess. There were intolerable production delays. While Shirley and I squabbled, the production crew stood idle, and it was worse when I was out of the country. In mid-season, Shirley made an unannounced flight to New York; the company was idled for a week. The overloaded camel's back finally broke. Lew Grade wisely aborted the show, two-thirds of the way through its commitment.

Well, you win some and you lose some.

The loss that really disturbed me was that of a series called *My World and Welcome to It*. Based on the writings and cartoons of James Thurber, it was innovative, adult, funny, and intelligent. It won the Emmy Award as the best new show of the 1969-70 season. It was canceled after twenty-six episodes. That says something about television, doesn't it?

ten

I Spying

I Spy was not merely a TV series. It was an adventure. It started at a luncheon table, in a restaurant high up in the NBC Building at Rockefeller Center. Mort Werner and Herb Schlosser, joint heads of programming for the network, had invited me to lunch, to see if we could get together on a series project. By accident rather than design, up to that point all of my output had gone to CBS or ABC. Werner and Schlosser asked me to come up with something for NBC.

For some time, I had been harboring a rather chancy notion, which I decided to try out on them. Television programming in the sixties had not evolved very far from the primitive, closeup-to-closeup techniques of its early days, when television screens were seldom larger than thirteen inches across, measured diagonally. The camera had to stay close, in order for the subject to be identifiable on the tiny screen. Although technological progress had been rapid and much larger screens were available, directors still clung to their outmoded, claustrophobic techniques.

Also, almost all television programs were limited to interior sets, because the cameras were bulky and relatively immobile. It didn't have to be that way. More compact, transportable equipment was available, but the filmmakers were slow to take advantage of the new technology, They had warehouses full of antiquated, but still usable, camera, sound, and lighting equipment. Why spend money for new stuff, when they could continue to take a depreciation credit on what they had?

I believed that we had been trapped on the sound stages by inertia. With the advent of sound, those huge structures had been built to shield the filming process from extraneous noise. They were still being used, long after the reasons for their use had disappeared.

I wanted to get out in the open. On the small screen, I wanted to put exotic locations that had seldom been seen, even on the big screen.

I told Schlosser and Werner that if they would give me a commitment for a full season, I would undertake to deliver a series such as television had not yet seen, except in travelogues, with exteriors filmed on locations all over the world. "Done!" they said, "subject to agreement on casting and premise."

The premise part was easy. The spy genre would yield opportunities for action and adventure and would give us the mobility I wanted. It could take us into obscure, picturesque corners of the world.

My protagonists would be a pair of attractive, athletic young men whose sense of humor would lighten the grim situations inherent in melodrama.

I knew just the writers who could handle that sort of stuff. Dave Friedkin and Mort Fine had written light-hearted adventure material for radio, and they had recently brought their typewriters over to the television studios. I pitched the idea to them, and they loved it. They signed on enthusiastically. We called the project *I Spy*.

NBC accepted the premise and gave us a commitment to go on the air, but in order to see how it worked on the screen, they specified that — in lieu of a pilot — a prototype episode be delivered for evaluation a month before the start of principal production. They also wanted the right to approve the casting of my two leads. Since that was okay with me, we had a deal.

The next priority was casting. We couldn't write for the leads until I knew who they were going to be. For one of the pair, I settled almost at once on Robert Culp, a talented actor-writer. Bob had come into my office some months earlier with a script, into which he had written a part for himself, very much like what we wanted for *I Spy*.

Bob is an attractive young man, who had been a college athlete. This was an important qualification for the part he was to play in *I Spy*. He would be doing a lot of climbing, running, fighting, jumping, and falling before the series had run its course.

It wasn't easy to find the other half of the spy team. We pored endlessly through casting directories. We needed some one who contrasted physically with Culp. We didn't want them looking like the Gold Dust Twins. (How many of you are old enough to remember *them*?) Our choice would have to have the same qualities of attractiveness, athleticism, and humor. We didn't find him in the casting directories, but one night I saw him on the television screen.

He was doing a stand-up comedy routine on a Jack Paar special.

He was handsome and animated, with a wonderfully mobile face. He was doing a comedy routine about karate; and he moved like an athlete. He was just what we needed for *I Spy*, except for one thing. He was black.

The day after I saw Bill Cosby on television, he walked in to visit with us at a *Van Dyke* reading. Carl's son, Rob, had also seen him on television. He told his father about Bill, so Carl had invited him to come to the studio, on the possibility that there might be something for him in the *Van Dyke Show*.

Not on your life! He belonged to me!

That same day, Bill was flying back to San Francisco, where he was playing an engagement at the Hungry i night club. I told Friedkin and Fine about him. Shortly thereafter, we flew to San Francisco to visit with him. While he played his night club engagement, Cosby and his wife, Camille, were living on a houseboat, anchored dockside in Sausalito.

We had a delightful visit on his houseboat. He showed us how to pierce the end of a cigar instead of cutting it. He told us about his undergraduate days at Temple. He reminisced about playing stick ball on the streets of Philadelphia. He charmed the pants off us!

That night we saw him work at the Hungry i, and after the show we got together with Roy Silver, Cosby's manager. I told him we wanted Cosby for *I Spy*. Because of the prevailing apprehension about the use of black actors, there might be some obstacles to overcome with the network, but if I could work that out, what kind of a deal could we make for Cosby's services? Silver said we could have him for twelve hundred and fifty dollars a show. You read me right. Bill Cosby for twelve-fifty a shot!

I said I'd let him know.

I flew to New York. In my carry-on luggage, I had a computer readout, analyzing the mail we had gotten after the *Van Dyke* episode in which Greg Morris had made a schmuck of Dick. It indicated that out of nineteen hundred and sixty pieces of mail, seventeen hundred and eighty two had applauded our presentation of the black man, two hundred and one were hostile, and the balance were indeterminate. I was prepared to claim that this showed the attitude of the viewing public was much more enlightened than it had been in the Amanda Randolph days.

The network brass would nevertheless be concerned that stations south of the Mason-Dixon line might defect. After all, a considerable part of the NBC network was south of Baltimore.

The computer readout was my ammunition for the battle I anticipated. I had reason to expect such questions as "You mean to say that these two fellas, the white man and a negra, are gonna go out on dates together? Sleep in the same room? Sit on the same toilet seat?"

I had a ten a.m. appointment with Robert Kintner, president of NBC, who had the contractual power of cast approval. Ten minutes before my appointment with Kintner, I dropped into Mort Werner's office. I made my pitch. I showed him pictures of Cosby and his resume. I told him about the mail reaction to the *Van Dyke* episode, and I asked for his support in my upcoming meeting with Kintner. He said he would back me up.

A few minutes later, in Kintner's office, we went through the standard amenities. "How do you want your coffee?"

"Black will be fine."

"How are things on the coast?"

"Just dandy."

Then, finally, "How's the casting coming along?"

"You know about Bob Culp. You okayed him."

"Yes. He'll be fine. How about the other part?"

"I haven't set anyone yet, but I've got my eye on someone."

"Oh? Do I know him?"

"No. He hasn't been around much, but I've seen his work, and he's just what I want."

"Then why don't you make a deal for him?"

"Because he's black."

"What difference does that make?"

I drew a long breath.

"As of this moment, Mr. Kintner, it makes no difference whatsoever!"

Friedkin and Fine came up with an intriguing plot for our prototype episode. Bob Culp would play Kelly Robinson, and Bill Cosby would be Alexander Scott. Kelly and Scott, ostensibly a professional tennis player and his trainer-manager, are actually agents of an unspecified department of the U.S. government, engaged in espionage. While playing in a tournament in Hong Kong, they are instructed to find a missing train that disappeared somewhere between the Chinese Border and Kowloon.

There was nothing of great monetary value on board, just building materials, bricks, mortar, and lumber. There was, however, an item of great strategic value — a shipment of weapons-grade plutonium.

Their search leads them to follow a newly-built spur of the railroad line into a Hakka village. The villagers are diligently constructing a school to replace the one that had recently burned down. They are using bricks, mortar, and lumber. An ancient lady nearby is watering her flowers with a long, snouted can, very much like the kind that engineers use to lubricate hard-to-reach parts of a locomotive. The workers are hoisting a school bell to the roof of their building. It strongly resembles the kind of bell one sees on the front of a locomotive.

After the required number of chases, bumps, and bruises, Kelly and Scott unravel the mystery. The villagers had built the spur from the railroad's main line and, with the cooperation of the crew, had hijacked the train, appropriated the building materials, and buried the train in a deep ditch they had dug. It now rests underground, with its cargo of deadly plutonium still on board. R.I.P.

In the spring of 1964, I took Culp, Cosby, and a basic crew to Hong Kong, to shoot the initial episode of *I Spy*. I didn't take picture-making equipment, because it would have been prohibitively expensive to ship it from L.A. to Hong Kong. I figured to rent what I needed from Run Run Shaw, the emperor of picture-making for the teeming oriental market.

He rented a full line of equipment to me, at what seemed to be a fair price. It turned out to be not so fair when everything we rented from him started to break down. He had given us the obsolete, ill-maintained stuff out of his studio warehouse, and we spent more time repairing it than using it. I vowed that, regardless of cost, I would never again depend on rented equipment.

We planned a seven-day shooting schedule, but we hadn't taken nature into consideration in our planning. On the second day, we were working on the Hong Kong side of the harbor, separated from our hotel on the Kowloon side, when the radio began to issue typhoon warnings. A typhoon in those latitudes is a serious matter, with winds exceeding a hundred and thirty miles per hour. The weather bureau makes sure that everyone receives plenty of warning when one is on the way. A flag is hoisted over the weather station in the harbor, warning all craft that a typhoon is in the geographical vicinity. Two flags mean that the typhoon is headed toward Hong Kong. Three flags mean that the storm is imminent, all traffic must cease, and all craft must seek shelter. Four flags mean "This is it, folks."

We were shooting in the Tiger Balm Gardens, a fantastic setting filled with plastic statues of gods and demons. It had been built by the enormously wealthy manufacturer of Tiger Balm, an extraordinary ointment reputed to cure everything from bunions to impotence. (You just rubbed it on the affected parts. No Chinese household would be without it. I tried it once on a sprained shoulder. Seconds after I rubbed it on my shoulder, I could taste it in my mouth. The taste didn't go away for days, and the smell! Wow!)

I was directing. Racing against the oncoming typhoon, with one eye on the flags over the weather station, I squeezed every last shot I could get out of the Tiger Balm Garden location. Rain started to come down in sheets, but that was all right with me. It gave the scenes a unique, eerie quality. We got our last shot just as the third flag went up. We caught the last Star Ferry to cross the harbor. There wasn't to be another craft on the water for the next five days.

I had a lovely suite on the top of the Peninsula Hotel, the Marco Polo Suite. It came complete with a kitchen, a dining room, and a butler named Benny. Benny kept a guest book. I signed my name under that of the Maharajah of Jaipur and two signatures down from Richard Nixon's.

The big windows overlooking the harbor had been boarded up to withstand the typhoon winds. Benny had a well-stacked refrigerator, and a talent for cooking. Unable to venture out of the hotel, Culp and Cosby joined me every morning for eggs benedict, or scrambled eggs with caviar. It was tough going, but we kept stiff upper lips.

We spent most of the five-day confinement staring out of the window at the turbulence below, and talking. In five days you can do a lot of talking.

Cosby told stories about his undergraduate days at Temple. Culp told about scripts he planned to write. I told about an incident that occurred on my honeymoon:

My bride and I had arrived at a cabin on Emerald Lake, in the Canadian Rockies. It was a blazing hot day. The thin air at eight thousand feet did nothing to modify the sun's vigor. The waters of the lake, just outside our cabin door, looked cool and inviting. I changed into swim trunks and dived in. I damned near died! The temperature of the water was barely above freezing! I should not have been surprised because I knew that the lake was fed by glacier melt. When I surfaced, I saw Frankie, my newly-wed wife, standing on the dock, looking hot and flustered. I decided to lure her in. It would be good for her. Invigorate her.

"Come on in," I told her. "The water's great. Very refreshing." She dived in, came up gasping, and I had to help her ashore. It was the last time I had her unqualified trust.

That incident, innocently related on a stormy afternoon, while we sipped Benny's excellent Bloody Marys, turned up in Cosby's first comedy album a year later. The band was called "Mr. and Mrs. Sheldon Leonard," and it went something like this:

"....He put a bathing suit on his gorgeous body, which has since turned bad on him....He sprang off the diving board with a lovely swan dive, and as he hit the water his body turned into a giant goose pimple.....He touched bottom and pushed up frantically, and as he rose through the icy water there was only one thought in his mind, and it was, 'Why should I tell her?'"

The record was a best seller, and to this day, millions of people regard me as a heartless sadist. So does my wife.

While we were immobilized by the typhoon, Bill's wife gave birth to their first child. I held Bill captive seven thousand miles away. I don't think Camille ever forgave me.

The typhoon finally cleared out. We finished the picture, and packed up. I had a minor problem. I had to figure out a way to cheat United States Customs.

The only exercise we could get during the typhoon had been walking through the many corridors of the Peninsula Hotel. One of them was a very seductive arcade, with windows displaying stunning merchandise at bargain prices. For four days, I walked past a window with a super-luxurious, black, vicuna topcoat on display. On the fifth day, I bought it. Flesh and blood can only stand so much.

Vicuna is an expensive item. The Customs Department would want a big cut. How could I cheat them?

On our return flight, we were scheduled to clear customs in Honolulu. I figured I could sneak my coat through customs by wearing it. They examine baggage, I thought, but they don't pay any attention to the clothes on your back.

The plane made its stop in Honolulu, and we lined up for customs. I was wearing my lovely, warm vicuna topcoat. The outside temperature was ninety-two degrees, with ninety percent humidity.

Sweat ran down my cheeks. Two paces behind me in the line, Bill bellowed, "Hey, Shel. You look warm. Why don't you take your coat off?"

The custom inspector's ears perked up.

"Yeah, Shel. You're sweating. Take off your coat."

I'll kill him! I thought. With my bare hands! I'll strangle him, and get Greg Morris to play the part!

By now I was facing the customs inspector. I had no alternative under the circumstances.

"I didn't list this coat," I told him. "Sorry. I just forgot to put it on my declaration. I bought it in Hong Kong."

"Yeah," he responded. "I was going to ask you about it, even before your friend started advertising. The first thing we look at is what people are wearing. You know, jewelry, vicuna coats.... They think they can get away with it, and they wind up in jail."

I paid the customs man. Cosby, the son of a bitch, had saved me from jail.

When we had edited, scored and titled the Hong Kong episode, we showed it to the NBC brass. They loved it, with one reservation. They didn't like Cosby. They wanted me to replace him.

It wasn't just that he was black, which was risky enough to start with, but his acting was amateurish. Unfortunately, that was true. His inexperience showed up on the screen.

"Don't worry," I told them. "He'll get better. He's a natural. This was his first shot at acting in front of a camera. Naturally, he was up tight, and I didn't have much time to help him. As soon as he relaxes he'll light up the screen."

"We still think you should replace him. There must be some guy out there who can do better. He doesn't have to be black.

"If you replace him, you better figure on replacing me, too."

"Oh...Well, if you feel that strongly...."

An enormous amount of preparation was required before we could start full-scale production on *I Spy*. Leon Chooluck, our location manager, along with Friedkin, Fine, and me, selected the cities we wanted to visit.

I prefer shooting in cities. The countryside and mountains of one country look very much like the countryside and mountains of any other country. It was Louis B. Mayer who said, when approached by a director who wanted to shoot in the Bernese Alps, "A rock is a rock. Shoot it in Griffith Park."

Cities have character. Not all cities, but many. Paris has character. Take a shot on any Parisian street, and any armchair traveler will place it immediately. The same is true for Venice, of course, and for London, Hong Kong, New York, Leningrad, Rio de Janeiro, Marrakesh, Istanbul, and a few others. It is not true for Berlin, Geneva, Belgrade, Tel Aviv, and many other cities, all of which look like Pittsburgh.

Once we had selected our location cities, we plotted six or more episodes for each location, in order to amortize the cost of the move. We still hadn't solved the equipment problem. I was determined not to depend on rented equipment, but transporting our own was hideously expensive. That's when Fuad Said came into the picture.

Fuad is an Egyptian. He is dapper, soft-spoken, and only a few inches more than five feet tall. When he came to me, he was just out of a course in cinematography at the University of Southern California. He had heard that I was going to make pictures in foreign countries, and he set out to convince me that I couldn't do it without him. He said that he would supply the equipment, personnel, location lunches, the whole package. I told him I couldn't take a chance on a guy with no experience. The next day he was back, with sixteen-millimeter film and a projector. He showed me pictures he had taken sky diving, with the camera built into his helmet, and pictures of sharks in a feeding frenzy, taken in twenty fathoms of Caribbean water. I chased him away, but day after day, he bounced back.

I told him that I couldn't talk with him about equipment and personnel, because I didn't know how I was going to handle that dilemma. He said he could solve it. He could build a vehicle, and load it with the smaller, lighter, more efficient equipment that was available: quartz lamps instead of bulky Sun Arcs; Arriflex cameras with nylon gears, instead of the heavier Mitchell cameras; small, efficient sound recorders; and airplane-style generators. He claimed that he could put all the equipment needed to make pictures under the most difficult conditions, night or day, into one modified Ford Econoline panel truck, small enough to be wheeled into the belly of a cargo plane and delivered the next day, anywhere in the world.

Fuad wore me down. Eventually, I advanced him the money to build the prototype vehicle of what would be known as the "Cinemobile".

The Cinemobile soon became indispensable for urban filming. Before the Cinemobile, when a company moved from one location spot to another, like from the Place Vendôme to Montparnasse, you had to move a whole fleet of trucks: the generator truck, the camera truck, the electrical truck, the prop truck, the sound truck, and a whole mess of etceteras. What with loading and unloading, fighting traffic, and struggling for parking spaces, a company could rarely make more than two moves a day. With the Cinemobile, we could make seven or eight moves. More importantly, we could use our own well-maintained equipment.

The Cinemobile was a lifesaver. Let me correct that. Little, persistent, indomitable Fuad Said was a lifesaver.

I directed most of the location sequences for *I Spy*, and the Cinemobile made the work relatively easy. The mobility it gave enabled me to hop around from spot to spot, squeezing the juices out of the rich foreign locations.

Because the pressure of office work relating to my other enterprises left me less time for directing, I enjoyed the rewards of directing on location even more. I always got more pleasure from directing than from any other activity connected with putting a show together, but increasing managerial responsibilities meant few directorial opportunities. Like the man said — there's no gain without pain.

eleven

The Inscrutable East

As we moved from country to country in the course of making *I Spy*, we became increasingly aware of difficulties that hadn't been taken into account when we were in pre-production. We discovered that every nation presented special problems because of the nature and culture of its people.

Hong Kong has more to offer the camera than almost any other city in the world, except Venice, Rio, and, perhaps, one or two other cities that I can't think of at the moment. In Hong Kong, wherever you look there is something flamboyant and exciting to brighten the screen. But while it offers wonderful backgrounds, it is certainly one of the most difficult places in the world in which to make pictures.

Crowd control is not a problem in all cities. In many of the busiest ones, people go about their business with no more than an over-the-shoulder glance at the picture makers. You can set up to film the return of Godzilla in the middle of Times Square or Piccadilly Circus, and the scurrying passersby will seldom turn a head.

In Hong Kong, however, as soon as you unload a motion picture camera, the word goes out and curious Asians come flocking in. The colony is inhabited by millions of people with very little to do. Its economy, though booming, can't absorb the endless flood of refugees from China and southeast Asia. Time hangs heavily on their hands. A picture company, with people going through incomprehensible but fascinating procedures — scurrying about, and performing mysterious tasks with reflectors and microphones — is free entertainment. It draws them like manure draws flies.

One of the first things we had done when we got to Hong Kong was to enlist the help and cooperation of the local police. They accompanied us to every location. I remember when we had set up to shoot a night scene in a remote back alley of Kowloon. During the day, we had slipped our equipment into the area in shopping bags, piece by piece, to foil the curious. As the day faded, we had remained happily undiscovered.

When it was dark enough, we got ready to shoot. The head electrician hit the generator switch. Our lights flooded the night sky. Ten minutes later, we were the center of a milling mob. The police got the crowd under control and pushed them behind an improvised rope barrier.

Just as we were ready to shoot, it started to rain. We cut the lights, covered the cameras, and repaired to a local coffeehouse to wait for the storm to pass, leaving an estimated five hundred people standing in the rain. Three hours later, at one o'clock in the morning, the rain stopped. We returned to our equipment, to find the five hundred rain-drenched looky-loos were still there.

We used many devices to foil the gawkers, but they seldom worked. Once, early in the morning, we placed a huge packing case, with a hinged flap on the side facing traffic, on the curb of busy Nathan Road. The plan was to sneak a camera and an operator into it, an hour or so before we were ready to shoot. We were going to have Culp and Cosby stroll innocently down Nathan Road, while the hidden camera filmed the scene. Wireless microphones would capture their dialogue. We hoped to get a completely natural-looking scene, with traffic flowing normally in the background, with nobody crowding into the foreground, nobody waving over Culp's shoulder, nobody thumbing his nose at the camera.

It might have worked, except that by the time we were ready to roll, the cameraman had passed out from the tropical heat in his little cage.

We tried installing a pane of one-way glass in the back of a panel truck, hoping we could shoot through it without advertising our presence. Unfortunately, the exterior surface of one-way glass acts as a mirror, so spectators happily preened and groomed themselves in it while our cameras rolled film.

One time, I desperately wanted to play a scene in front of the dazzling facade of a restaurant on Boundary Road, in the bustling heart of Kowloon. The restaurant had a gorgeous, sixty-foot-long, crimson dragon mounted over its entrance. The wall alongside was festooned with a structure of bamboo and reeds, which was a platform for the workmen who were repairing the building wall. The whole thing was supported by sturdy bamboo poles. It looked wonderfully Oriental. I hungered to get it on film.

There was a public toilet across the street from the restaurant. We disguised our crew in laborers' clothes. We broke down the camera and tripod and put the parts in baskets, which, with the crew, we smuggled onto the roof of the toilet, well out of public view. In the scene we were about to play, the villains were instructed to drive around a corner onto Boundary Road, with Culp and Cosby in a second car, close behind. The villains were to pull up in front of the restaurant, get out of the car, and pause for a moment to allow my camera to gloat over the gorgeous crimson dragon. Then they were to enter the restaurant, followed by our boys. Sounds simple, right? But the preparation that preceded it would have been appropriate for the D-Day landings on Omaha Beach.

Because we wanted an experienced man at the wheel — one who would be sure to hit the exact mark in front of the restaurant — we pressed the driver of the Cinemobile into service, as the driver of the lead car. Each car carried a high-powered receiver for our radioed instructions. We timed the traffic lights, so that we could send the cars into the intersection on a green light. We walked our actors through the scene, so they could see the marks they were expected to hit. Through it all, nobody paid any attention to us. Victory was in sight!

When everything was ready, I crossed my fingers and radioed the signal for action. The lead car came in to the scene and made the turn onto Boundary Road smoothly, Culp and Cosby close behind. Things were going fine. The pedestrian flow was uninterrupted. As the first car drove up to the restaurant, edged toward the curb, and slid up to its mark, the side mirror clipped one of the bamboo poles that supported the workers' platform, knocking it out of place. The whole thing came tumbling down. Workers rolled on the sidewalk, screaming and cursing. Pedestrians crowded around. People flooded out of nearby buildings. Within moments, everybody this side of Pasadena had jammed into the scene.

We worked on rooftops and hillsides, where none before us had ventured. We shot in squatter colonies that were controlled by the Triad, the Chinese equivalent of the Mafia. The crime lords assigned specific areas of crime to each colony, and nobody dared trespass on their franchise. One colony might be given the exclusive right to roll drunken sailors in the Suzy Wong district; another might be given the right to blackmail shopkeepers; another might have protection rights over the gambling houses; still another might get prostitution.

These colonies were made up of the refugees who had flooded into Hong Kong faster than they could be absorbed. On the hillsides, they put up flimsy shelters, made of packing cases and corrugated cardboard. The narrow passageways between hovels were ankle-deep in mud.

I remember that aspect well, because of an incident with Cosby.

I was directing a scene in which he is being chased by a Chinese villain who is close behind him, firing a pistol. Cosby simulates being shot and falls to the wet ground at a designated spot, according to a plan previously arranged with Culp. The pursuer rushes into the scene to make sure of his hit; as he stands over his fallen victim, Culp springs out of a nearby hiding place and shoots him. The villain falls dead. That's the way it was planned. This is what actually happened.

We couldn't rehearse the scene, because once Cosby fell in the mud, it would take a lot of time to clean him up and put him in a fresh wardrobe. We went for an unrehearsed take.

It went well, up to a point. Cosby dashed in, pretended to be shot, and dropped, face down, into the malodorous mud. A pig that was living in a nearby packing case stuck his snout out and nosed the fallen man, bless his little porky heart! An ad libbing pig!

The villain appeared, Culp popped out of his hiding place and bang! bang! The villain spun around like a top, four times, staggered around a while, lurched over to a rock, and sat on it!

"Cut!" I screamed. "What the hell goes on here?"

I called for the interpreter.

"Has the guy gone crazy?" I asked. "All he's got to do is fall down. What's with the ballet performance? Does he think he's Baryshnikov? Straighten him out. Clean Cosby up, and we'll try it again. Please God, let that lovely pig do what he did, once more."

On Take Two, Cosby and the pig performed flawlessly. The villain came into the scene and got shot. He fell to the ground, as instructed, stuck his leg up in the air like a goddam flagpole and wobbled it about!

"Cut! Cut! Cut! Gimme a gun! A real gun! I'll kill him! I'll teach him how to die! What is it with him?"

The interpreter explained, "He doesn't want to make it look too real, as though he's really dead, because if the demons think he's helpless, they will steal his soul."

Well, you can't argue with that.

Take Three. Cosby came into the scene and fell into the mud. The pig did his thing. What a ham! The villain rushed in and Culp shot him. He staggered out of the shot, presumably to die off screen. All's well that ends well.

Fuad Said was an important factor in making the location a success. The hastily assembled crew, under his guidance, worked as though they had been together for years. The equipment he supplied worked flawlessly, because he often stayed up all night to service and maintain it. The location lunches he provided would have done credit to a gourmet restaurant. Pâtés, salads, a choice of lobster, chicken, or roast beef, and a choice of beverages — Coca-Cola or Mouton Rothschild — to wash it all down.

When I told Said what kind of shot I wanted, no matter how difficult it was, his invariable answer was "No problem."

One time, I needed a shot from the roof of the Peninsula Hotel, looking down into the courtyard. Fuad went up to the roof to line it up. I followed a short time later. I saw a startling sight. Fuad was hanging over the end of a two-by-twelve plank, balanced like a seesaw, over a parapet twelve stories above the courtyard. With Fuad at one end, the other end was balanced by a scrawny Chinese boy. He got the shot I had asked for. Later he explained that the precarious device was the only way he could get over the parapet, because there was a wide drainage ditch separating it from the rest of the roof. It was a lucky day for me when he came to my office and began twisting my arm.

Despite the problems, we left Hong Kong loaded with cinematic goodies. Fuad Said stole some shots with a hand-held camera in a gambling parlor, amid the deafening click, click, click of mah-jongg tiles. We got shots in the red-light district, with prostitutes glowering at us from every window. We shot stuff on Cat Street, where the shopkeepers hid their faces whenever the camera turned their way. The city officials were marvelously helpful. The unfailingly cooperative Hong Kong police got us into places we hadn't dared hope to see — places that had never before been filmed.

Since the mid-sixties, when we worked in Hong Kong, many film companies have taken advantage of the extraordinary variety of backgrounds it offers. However, we were one of the early ones.

Japan was our next foreign location. In Japan, crowd control is not a big problem. The industrious Japanese are inclined to go about their affairs, and the fact that they are jammed together in living quarters separated from one another by paper partitions has trained them to mind their own business. Many of the problems we encountered in Japan were caused by the national personality.

I had visited Japan for the first time in 1953, when the Japanese were uniformly helpful and cooperative and eager to please. They were still recovering from the trauma of World War II, and they wanted to regain acceptance.

When I came back with the *I Spy* company in 1966, they had changed. In the intervening years, Japan had prospered mightily. They were no longer humble and ingratiating. The old Imperial arrogance was reappearing.

They reneged on agreements. They raised previously agreed-upon prices. With some notable exceptions, such as Ian Mutsu, grandson of one of Japan's revered Prime Ministers, who was our expeditor, they were unfriendly and unhelpful.

Nikko, a village an hour train ride out of Tokyo, is a collection of marvelous, legendary temples. We had scheduled four days of shooting there and had reservations in the local hotel, for five actors and a crew of twenty. We arrived to find that our reservations had been canceled to make room for a convention of industrialists. The hotel manager made no apology. Our location manager scattered the company around in private homes, which made it difficult to gather everybody together for the start of the day's work. We fell two days behind schedule.

We were shooting in a fishing village on the Izu peninsula when we ran into a unique problem. The local people had taken offense at our presence, for reasons we never determined. The bare-breasted women of the village kept walking into our shots, thrusting their well-developed bosoms at the camera. I liked the effect, but the network censors would have been unhappy.

In this same fishing village, Mort Fine stepped into an open sewer drain, up to his knee. He claims that since then his right foot is two shoe sizes larger than his left foot.

We had made arrangements to shoot in Tokyo's huge central market, in the section where tons and tons of freshly frozen fish are unloaded every day. When we arrived on the scheduled day and started to unload, we were turned away. It seems the management had second thoughts. They had decided that the heat of our lamps might thaw their frozen fish.

I wasn't sorry to leave Japan, even though they have excellent beer.

twelve

South of the Border

Our Mexican location was a ball, largely due to the hospitality of Frank Brandstetter, managing director of the Las Brisas Hotel in Acapulco. Nicknamed Brandy, he is a good-looking man, athletically built, of medium height, and slightly balding. He is one of the world's best hoteliers. The hotel chain with which he was associated had sent him to Mexico to take over the reorganization and operation of Las Brisas. He whipped a gang of semi-illiterate locals into a skilled, smoothly-operating staff. Competing hotels constantly grabbed his waiters, bellmen, and doormen, and upped them to managerial positions. He made me and my company feel welcome and pampered.

For the benefit of those unfortunates who have never been there, Las Brisas is a collection of *casitas*, nestled in the side of a mountain, overlooking the bay of Acapulco. Each *casita* has a private swimming pool, and a little pink jeep with which to negotiate the winding hill road that gives access to the *casitas*. Every morning, when you rub the sleep out of your eyes and open the door of your *casita* to the glorious panorama that lies before you, on your doorstep you will find a basket of crisp, freshly-baked rolls (the Mexicans are unexcelled when it comes to breads and rolls), a bowl of fresh fruit, and a thermos of coffee.

Brandstetter was under the mistaken impression that I had once saved his life. The hotel guests lunched, sunned, and bathed in the swimming cove called La Concha. Few swimmers ventured outside the cove, because of the surging water that would carry a swimmer halfway into the cove and then sweep him out again.

165

Although he was a competent swimmer, the first time Brandstetter swam out of the cove, he didn't know how to manage the surge. I was also outside, snorkeling, and I could see that he was struggling. He would muscle half-way into the cove, only to be swept back by the retreating waters. Wearing fins, it was easy for me to come to his assistance and help him into the cove. It was as simple as that, but from that day on, I was a favored guest at Las Brisas. Brandstetter couldn't do enough for me. The beauty of Las Brisas and Brandstetter's warm hospitality made Acapulco one of our most enjoyable locations.

In this case, his hospitality was repaid. For weeks, we shot film in and around Las Brisas. When the resulting episodes were broadcast, millions of people all over America saw our heroes dashing about a tropical paradise in their saucy pink jeeps, prominently labeled with the Las Brisas logo, or splashing around in their secluded, private swimming pool. It didn't do Las Brisas a bit of harm.

Mexicans have a carefree attitude toward reservations. Not once but several times our location manager approached the reservation desk of a hotel or airline to check the company in, only to find that the clerk had never heard of us and had no record of our arrangements. He would remain blandly unconvinced in the face of letters of confirmation and deposit receipts, but after a discreet exchange of pesos, he was likely to find our reservations tucked away in an overlooked file.

Mexican cuisine covers the culinary spectrum from delicious to deadly. Soups are a Mexican specialty, and the seafood, particularly freshly-caught crab and shrimp, is wonderful. Their hot foods are really, really hot! *Jalapeno* peppers can turn your mouth into a disaster area for hours. The beer is excellent, but the water is generally undrinkable. Since the dishes are washed in it, and the ice for drinks is made with it, *La Turista*, or "Montezuma's revenge" is unavoidable. There are all sorts of medications available for it, but none of them do much good — the damn thing must run its five- or six-day course. There is an oft-told story about the Mexican tourist visiting up North, who complained that American drinking water gave him constipation!

Characteristically, the Mexican people are anxious to please. If you ask a question, a Mexican is likely to give you the answer he thinks you want to hear — which is not necessarily the hundred-per-cent-true answer.

For instance: "Is it very far to Taxco?"

"No, *señor*. Is not far."

"That's too bad. I wanted to make an all-day trip, but if it's so close..."

"Oh, no, *señor*. Is not too close. Is pretty far."

This otherwise engaging trait can cause trouble. I needed a freshly-caught sailfish for a scene we were shooting in Acapulco. Getting one wasn't a problem. The fleet of sport-fishing boats came in every afternoon, loaded with triumphant tourists, eager to string up their finny victims and have their picture taken. For a few pesos, after it had been well-photographed with its conqueror, the conqueror's wife, his nephew Albert, and all three of them together, we bought a nice hundred-and-forty-pound sailfish.

The light was getting yellow. I said to Tony Morales, our Mexican first assistant, "If we can't get a shot before the sun goes down, the fish will have to keep until morning. Will that be all right?"

"Oh, sure. We'll keep it tied up in the water. It'll be fine. Don't worry."

That's the national motto, "Don't worry."

The next morning, we hauled our moored fish out of the water. The crabs had gotten to it overnight. Our hundred-and-forty-pound sailfish had become forty pounds of bone and gristle. We blew a whole day's work while we waited for the boats to come in with another fish.

But rest assured that when it comes to working or vacationing in Mexico, the pluses far outnumber the minuses.

Earle Hagen, the brilliant conductor-composer who did the scoring for all of my films, had heard of a unique kind of music, played by bands that called themselves *Chiles Fritos*. They could only be heard in the remote villages buried in the hills of the State of Guerrero. Acapulco is in Guerrero, but incredible as it may seem, just a few miles from that glamorous, sophisticated city is a primitive, untamed country into which even the *Rurales* dare not venture singly.

Brandstetter volunteered to send a messenger into the hills to collect a musical group from one of the buried villages, so that Earle could record their sound for background music. The messenger brought back eight musicians. Their instruments had been confiscated from the Emperor Maximillian's military bands, as fruits of the nineteenth-century revolution which freed Mexico from foreign domination and led to Maximillian's execution.

Clad in loose-fitting, clean, white, pajama-like garments, some of them bare-footed and some wearing sandals, they were ushered into Brandy's living room. They were quiet, shy, simple men, ranging in age from thirty to forty. Bewildered by their surroundings, their eyes darted from side to side, taking in everything. When Earle explained that he wanted to record them, they were eager to cooperate.

They had never been recorded and, in fact, had probably never heard a recording. The instruments they carried — percussion, brass, and woodwinds — were genuine antiques which had been passed from generation to generation. Untaught, the musicians had experimented with their instruments, until they could produce the sounds they wanted. They were farmers who would work their farms during the day, and, when the sun set, would wash up, put on clean clothes, and get together for a practice session. They were called upon when there was a wedding, a christening, a funeral, or any occasion that could be brightened by music. They were not paid with cash but were plied with food and drink, and they enjoyed great prestige in their village.

They played for us. None of them had ever seen a sheet of music, and the sounds they produced were like nothing we had ever heard before. When we played the recording back for them they were hypnotized. They liked it. They exchanged congratulatory glances. At the end of the session, Earle offered to pay them. They were indignant. One does not accept money for doing what one does for the love of doing it. The whole incident was so very Mexican.

Earle also used his recorder to good effect with the ubiquitous *mariachis*. The term *"mariachi"* is a corruption of the word "marriage." Every evening the itinerant bands play in designated areas of the principal cities. Those who want to hire musicians to play at a wedding or any festive occasion come to the square to make a selection from among the dozen or more competing bands.

Due to Earle's diligence with his recorder, the background music for *I Spy* always authentically ethnic.

We were shooting in Guadaljara when the Seven-Day War broke out in Israel. On the morning of the day after Israel trashed the Egyptian army, destroying their ground and air forces, Fuad Said approaced Friedkin, Fine, and me, his three Jewish bosses, as we were standing in the huge Central Market planning camera setups.

"Today all the shots will be out of focus." he said, and stalked away.

Guanajuato is a marvelously interesting city, deep in the heart of colonial Mexico. When Spain ruled Mexico, Guanajuato was the most important silver mining area in the world. To this day its hills are honeycombed with abandoned mining tunnels. The city is beautiful. Quaint and unspoiled, it is likely to remain that way until, discovered by tourists, it acquires a McDonald's franchise. As of now, there are no souvenir shops and the people are gentle and courteous.

On Saturday nights, the young people dress up in their finest and gather together in the *Zocalo*, the town square. The young men parade around the square in a clockwise direction, while the girls go around counterclockwise. It is a wonderful arrangement for mutual inspection, and shy glances from under lowered lids.

In Guanajuato, we spent several days shooting in what is probably the most unusual setting for filmmaking to be found anywhere in the world: The ancient mining tunnels under the city have been turned into catacombs lined with mummies!

Level ground is at a premium in the hills which shelter Guanajuato, and the level ground needed for a cemetery is restricted to a sparse acre and a half cut into a hillside. In colonial days, burial plots were not sold but were rented for a negotiated period of years, after which the occupant was disinterred to make room for a waiting customer.

Although this custom was nationwide in the hilly areas of Mexico, in Guanajuato it took on a unique, macabre character. When the bodies were disinterred from the mineral-rich soil of Guanajuato, they were found to be perfectly preserved, even after many years of burial. The unprecedented mummification was due to the chemistry of the soil.

What to do? Once you took the tenant out of his grave, where did you put him? He had not conveniently turned into dust and ashes, which could be disposed of without a second thought. There he was, looking pretty much the way he had on the day he was buried.

The city fathers solved the problem by installing the dear departed in niches cut into the walls of the city's many abandoned mining tunnels. There they stand to this day, in the dim light of the catacombs, in the garb and the posture in which they had been buried.

There is a lady who died in childbirth, with her still-born babe cradled in her arms. There is the man killed in a mining accident, with his decapitated head balanced on his shoulders. There is one tenant of the catacombs whose posture suggests a grim conclusion: she was buried with her hands sedately folded on her bosom, but when they dug her up, her arms were flung wildly over her head.

Since the city officials did not object to our using the mortuary chambers as a set, we shot great sequences there. The fact is that the Mexicans take a realistic, unsentimental attitude toward death. Their cemeteries are not grim forests of granite memorials. Their headstones are painted in pastel colors, and ornamented with plaster cherubs. Each year, on the Day of the Dead, families come to the cemeteries to picnic on the graves of departed relatives. As they eat and drink, they feel the presence of the dead, and they welcome it. It is not a sad occasion. Children play on the graves. There is laughter and singing. Shops are filled with articulated skeleton toys. Beer is drunk out of skull-shaped goblets. It is possible that the impoverished, overworked, ordinary people of Mexico consider death a happy release.

Culp and Cosby had been injecting a lot of ad-libs into their work lately. Most of it was good, very good, in fact. No less could be expected of Bob Culp, who had a talent with words, and Bill Cosby, who was a world-class champion at that kind of stuff. However, ad-libs can be dangerous. It's easy to be amused by a witty ad lib and to overlook the damage it's doing to do to the structure of the tale you're telling.

The ad-lib problem with Culp and Cosby had been developing for some time. It had started innocently enough. Bill's natural speech pattern was studded with interjections. A line of dialogue such as "I can't do a thing like that!"

coming from him would naturally and gracefully become "Hey, that ain't the kind of thing I can do, man!"

So far, so good. Allowing Bill the liberty of adjusting his dialogue eased his transition from being a stand-up comic to being an actor.

Bob Culp was a big help in that regard. He undertook to tutor Bill in the fundamentals of acting for the camera. Bob, an intelligent, articulate man, is a fine craftsman in several creative areas, and he was an important factor in Bill's early development. Ironically, early in the second year of *I Spy's* run, his success in helping Bill began to backfire.

As soon as *I Spy* went on the air, Bill Cosby gained sensational acceptance. He became the darling of the critics. Fan mail poured in. His fee as a night club performer skyrocketed. After his first year on the air, he won an Emmy as the best actor in a TV series. As he gained self-assurance in front of the camera, his natural charm came through irresistibly.

But while the warm sun of public approval was shining on Bill, Bob was lingering in the shadows. He had been the teacher and Bill had been his pupil. But then an ironic role reversal began. Bob started interpolating "Hey, man," "real cool," and "groovy" into his dialogue.

The carefully designed characterizations of the two leads, contrasting but complementing each other, became homogenized. What had started as harmless interjections became increasingly intrusive ad-libs, often inconsistent with the story line.

Eventually it reached the point where they were totally unacceptable. An episode was shot in Guanajuato in which Gene Hackman, as a recently released criminal, has set a diabolical trap to destroy Jim Backus, the F.B.I. agent who had sent him to prison. Culp and Cosby chase the Hackman character into the surrounding hills and wound him fatally in a gun battle. The dying criminal gloatingly tells them that they are too late. He has already loaded the piñata hanging in Backus's living room with nitroglycerine. It is Christmas morning, and when the sun rises, Backus's children will be blindfolded and given clubs that they will swing wildly, trying to break the piñata. When a club strikes it, it will burst, but instead of showering down gifts and candy, it will shower down death.

"It's too late to stop it," the dying culprit boasts. "Sunrise is less than an hour away, and you're eighty miles from town."

What follows is the standard Race Against Death. Halfway to the goal, the car they're driving sputters to a stop, out of gas. Culp turns to Cosby and, in his best Oliver Hardy manner, snarls, "This is another fine mess you've gotten us into, Stanley."

Our two heroes are barreling down the mountainside to save innocent children from destruction, the suspense building with every turn of the wheels. Backus and his three kids are about to be blown to bits and they're making jokes! "This is another fine mess you've gotten us into, Stanley!"

I wasn't on the location when the bit in question was shot, but I saw it two days later in the projection room. I sent a second unit back to Mexico to re-shoot it with doubles, a correction that cost the show twenty thousand dollars.

The most serious problem arising from our Mexican location — aside from brushes with corrupt officials, swarming insects, grasping reservation clerks, and unsafe drinking water — developed after we had wrapped principal photography.

It was our custom to hire many of the actors we needed for supporting parts in the location country. This saved transportation and per diem costs, and gave us authentic characterizations. Frequently, an actor we had hired abroad had to be brought to Hollywood to finish his part in studio interiors. When we sought to bring our Mexican actors to Hollywood, we ran into a real roadblock. U.S. Immigration wouldn't let them into the country.

There is an unacknowledged collaboration between the Screen Actor's Guild and the Immigration Service. When a foreign actor seeks to enter the U.S., Immigration officers call the Guild to get their opinion as to whether the actor's services are indispensable and irreplaceable. In our case, the Guild's response was that with plenty of Latino actors here who could use the work, keep the wetbacks out. We couldn't finish our Mexican episodes without the actors who had already begun their roles. An expensive, time-consuming battle ensued before we were able to cajole, threaten, and entreat effectively enough to get the actors we needed into the country.

I am fond of Mexico. It is a country with many faces. There are the bustling, sleazy border towns, like Tijuana and Juarez. There are dazzling resorts on the Pacific coast and on the Yucatan Peninsula, quiet country towns, prosperous modern cities with stunning architecture, the Aztec pyramids of Teotihuacan, the Mayan ruins of Chichen Itza and Monte Alban, and villages deep in the hills, untouched by the twentieth century. There are the Floating Gardens of Xochimilco, and fishing villages where the fishermen stand waist deep in the surf to cast baited hooks to the swarming sharks. A company could shoot pictures there for years and not begin to make use of all Mexico has to offer.

I can't leave Mexico without another story about Frank Brandstetter. His past was shrouded in mystery. It was plain that he had done something important in the military during World War II. Admirals and generals visited with him in Acapulco. Astronauts were his guests. The first men on the moon named a crater after him.

In the course of time, I picked up a few interesting fragments of his background. He once showed me a clipping from *The New York Times* pertaining to an incident during the war, that had been suppressed by the British Official Secrets Act. Such coverage expires after twenty years, unless renewed, and the twenty-year period had passed. The article reported that Brandstetter had been with the counter-intelligence branch of the armed forces, and, being multi-lingual, had become the chief interrogator of prisoners of war held in England. His job was to pry as much information as he could out of them. A prisoner's indiscreet response could sometimes provide valuable information about the nature and disposition of enemy forces.

Brandstetter practiced interrogation as a science, making a judgment about each subject's strengths and weaknesses. He flattered the vain, reassured the timid, intimidated the cowardly, and praised the boastful.

Late in the war, he was on leave in London one weekend when he received urgent orders to report to headquarters, to be confronted with a prime mystery. There were four POW camps scattered about in the south of England. Earlier in the day, eleven prisoners, dispersed among the four camps, had staged a simultaneous breakout. All were high-ranking officers. That they could have broken out wasn't surprising, as security in such camps was less than tight. After all, the men were deep in enemy country, and once they got beyond the restraining barbed wire, where could they go? Yet it was obvious that outside forces must have been at work to synchronize the breakouts. The unanswered question was: Why?

Two days later, the mystery deepened. The eleven high-ranking officers all returned simultaneously. Something very strange was taking place, and it was Brandy's job to find out what it was.

Day after day, Brandy probed and pried at his subjects. After two weeks, he found a vulnerable spot in the makeup of a young, homosexual major. At one point, the major revealed his concern for his lover, who was also a prisoner. That was all Brandy needed. He threatened to stage an escape attempt, during which the major's lover would be killed. He faked phone calls to confederates, planning the details of the lover's murder. He was very convincing. Soon, the tortured major poured out the details of the plot that lurked behind the breakout.

German intelligence agents had smuggled instructions from the German High Command to the officers, instructing them to escape at an indicated time and rendezvous at an indicated place. Once there, they were told to return to their respective prisons and organize their fellow prisoners for a major escape. On a predetermined day, at a given signal, a diversion would be created outside the confines of each prison: A fire would break out in a nearby building. In the ensuing confusion, the officers were to lead their men in a mass breakout. They were then to proceed to a place where they would find a cache of weapons, and, now armed, they were to march on London, threatening to attack the city.

The purpose? By timing the attack to occur when the German High Command was planning an offensive in the Ardennes Forest, they hoped to divert English troops away from the front, for the defense of London.

I thought the story was fascinating, and I thought it would make a hell of a movie. It took it to CBS, in the person of a recently-appointed Head of Special Programs. The young man told me that, while it was an interesting story, it wouldn't make a good movie because the audience would identify and empathize with the wrong element.

"You mean with the prisoners?"

"Sure. They always sympathize with the underdog."

"Even when the underdogs are Nazis who want to get out so they can kill a lot of our guys?"

"Oh, sure."

That young man, with the ink still wet on his diploma from the Ypsilanti College of the Performing Arts, was in charge of spending millions of dollars for his network.

Dining was important to me when I was on location. It made a great difference when the day's work was done. When we started making *I Spy*, I went on the locations without my wife. Each day, when we wrapped up our scheduled work, I'd go back to the hotel, shower and change, order a Martini from room service, and decide how I was going to spend the hours until bedtime. Should I join the guys, who were organizing a poker game? Should I sit at a sidewalk table on the Via Veneto and watch the people passing by, while I ate pasta and drank cappuccino? Or should I just say "The hell with it," and call room service for a club sandwich and a bottle of beer?

Starting with the Mexican locations, I persuaded my wife to come with me. It made a difference in my after-work habits. She was waiting for me at the end of the day. I would shower and change, then, following the advice of the concierge, we'd go to a fine restaurant, have a cocktail and a leisurely dinner, an after-dinner brandy, then saunter back to the hotel, with the memory of an evening well-spent. It made the day complete.

Because having my wife with me made long location stays more tolerable, and because I wanted the members of my cast and crew to share the same privilege, I encouraged them to bring their spouses along. We increased the per diem allowance for those who were joined by their spouses. We made hotel and travel arrangements accordingly. Instead of being mere nutrition, dinner became an anticipated occasion.

Three or four couples would go to dinner together. Frequently the highlight of the evening was watching Cosby

177

eat. Oh, boy! He is a fabulous athlete with a knife and fork. He enjoys food. The extraordinary thing about it was that he could put on ten or more pounds, then, almost magically, shed them whenever he so decided.

Years after *I Spy*, he and I were making a Movie of the Week for NBC in Rome. A car and driver would wait for us each morning at daybreak to take us to the location. Cosby would come bouncing down the hotel steps to join me in the car. He never said "Good morning." His greeting was "Where are we going to eat tonight?"

To this day, when I drop into Piccolo Mondo or Taverna Flavia or other fine Roman restaurants, they ask me when Cosby is coming back. He paid off their mortgages.

In the course of filming *I Spy*, we worked in fourteen countries. We would spend a month, more or less, in each country, filming the exterior scenes for a package of five or six scripts. Each country left me with memories.

I remember it was in Spain that Bill Cosby was able to indulge his taste for fine, hand-rolled, Cuban cigars, unavailable in the States and the other countries that boycott Cuban products. They are considered to be the finest cigars in the world, partly because of the quality of the leaf, but mostly because of the skill of the cigar makers, to whom the tradition of cigar-making is passed from generation to generation. The cigars were available in Madrid, but they weren't cheap.

In Spain, I also remember attempting to shoot a scene on a ranch that bred fighting bulls for the arena. Back in Hollywood, it had seemed like a good idea. Culp and Cosby would be pursued across the pastures of the ranch, eluding the charges of the fierce, bellowing, fighting bulls, as well as their pursuers.

What do you do when you discover that when they are in the herd fighting bulls are as placid as cows? They won't bellow and snort, and they won't charge. They're too busy grazing, and doing the things that bulls do to cows. So what do you do?

You rewrite, that's what you do.

When you've finished the rewrite, instead of being chased across the bull ranch pasture, the boys are being chased across the high-arched aqueduct in Segovia.

In Germany, I remember how eager the young people were to erase our memories of their fathers and grandfathers.

I wanted to scout a possible location on the grounds of a castle in Kronberg, twenty miles out of Frankfurt. My location manager had arranged for a car and driver to meet us at the railroad station, but they weren't there when we got off the train. We waited. A half hour passed, and still no car. After a while, we called the office of the car hire company. The office manager was shocked.

"Didn't the station master tell you? We called an hour ago and left a message with him. We left a telephone number you should call for another car, because our car was damaged in an accident."

The station master's office was only a few steps from where we had been waiting. I rapped on his window. "Why didn't you tell us that our car wasn't coming?"

"I am not a messenger boy for goddam Americans!" he told me.

Then I told him some things — like what kind of four-legged farm animal was his mother and what particular species of ape was his father. He slammed his window down.

A little cluster of local teenagers had been listening to the altercation. They were obviously disturbed.

"Don't be mad," one of them told me. "He was in the war. His wife was killed in a bombing raid. You must forgive him."

Another one said, "I will help you. I will get my father's car."

"If you want to go to the castle," a girl volunteered, "there is a short cut through the woods. It is a pleasant walk. We will take you."

In school, they were all studying English as their second language, and they were eager to befriend us. They made me hopeful for Germany's future.

In England, I remember when we were shooting in the garden of a rural pub. We had hired a well-known British actor who in the course of the scene was required to down a pint of ale. We couldn't fake it with cold tea, because the foaming head of the brew was very visible to the camera.

The cameras rolled. The actor swilled down his pint of ale. As the last drops trickled down his throat, the camera operator yelled, "Cut! It's no good. A cloud came over the sun, and the light changed. We need another take."

Well, these things happen. Roll 'em for Take Two. Another pint, and another cloud. Take Three and Pint Three, followed by Pints Four, Five, Six, and Seven, punctuated by trips to the W.C. We got the shot on the seventh take, and the actor staggered off the set to a hearty round of applause. He went home, popped into bed, and didn't move a muscle for twenty-four hours.

In Morocco, I remember the tradition of fine cuisine, left over from the years of French occupation. The heritage of French culinary artistry, combined with the rich variety of Moroccan produce, makes many Moroccan cities a gourmet's delight.

Cosby dined well in Morocco. So did we all. But I remember some less pleasant things about Morocco. We were damned near blind. If you opened your mouth, you might lose the gold fillings in your teeth. The thieves would take anything that wasn't nailed down. So help me, they even stole reflectors which are five-foot-by-five-foot squares, painted with glistening silver paint to reflect sunlight to the areas the cameraman wants to brighten. Although they are of no possible use to anyone but a cameraman, three of them were stolen.

We had cast Maurice Evans, one of England's finest actors, as a Moroccan nobleman, garbed in caftan, *djellaba*, and red shoes with turned-up toes. Because Maurice had foot trouble, he had to wear specially-made orthopedic shoes. Between takes, when he relaxed, he took off the fancy red shoes and put on his comfortable orthopedics. He would change back when he was called for the scene. He changed back and forth twice. He couldn't change a third time, because by then his orthopedic shoes were stolen. The poor man limped through the balance of the day in his red shoes.

Fortunately, he had a reserve pair of his special shoes that he brought to the set on the second day. They lasted until just before the lunch break.

He had one more pair. He brought them to the set on the third day, and I paid a local urchin a few coins to stand guard over them. The kid stole them. During the rest of his stay with us, Maurice Evans, distinguished actor, sophisticated gentleman, wore a pair of sneakers with his dinner clothes.

It was difficult to enlist satisfactory "atmosphere people" from among the locals. They were slow to understand instructions, which had to be relayed to them through interpreters. In many cases, superstitions made them reluctant to appear in front of the camera. It was easier to press a couple of our wives into service.

I cherish the memory of Cosby on a camel that was led by two unlikely-looking Arabs, one of whom bore a striking resemblance to my blonde wife, while the other looked very much like Mrs. Cosby.

The Moroccan police were brutal toward their own people, and obsequious toward us. I remember putting a wide-eyed, ten-year-old boy into a shot on the spur of the moment. I had seen him washing his feet in a public fountain, and I thought that would make a nice piece of business in the foreground. Through our interpreter, he was told what he was to do when the cameras rolled. He performed flawlessly. I gave him a few Moroccan francs and told him he could share our lunch. The kid could hardly contain himself. If you had never before seen a boy walking on a cloud, here was your chance.

When we went back to work after lunch, he considered himself a member of the company. When one of the policemen who accompanied us ordered the spectators back behind a restraining rope, the boy didn't think the order applied to him. The policeman thought differently. With his baton, he walloped the kid across his back, knocking him to his knees.

I saw the whole thing, and it made me very mad. The policeman couldn't understand my anger. He had just been doing his job. What was all this fuss about nearly killing a mere native boy?

When we finished up in Morocco, I had mixed feelings. I was glad to get away from the oppressive atmosphere of an absolute monarchy, but I knew that I would always remember the excitement of the medina in Fez, the drama of the Square of the Dead in Marrakesh, the sophistication of Casablanca, the majesty of the Atlas Mountains, the Blue Men down from the hills, the Berbers with their ancient rifles, the muezzins calling the faithful to worship, the clamor of the camel market, the stink of the tanning pits, and the ever-present dope peddlers offering the very best hashish, effendi, very cheap.

Morocco was an exciting, stimulating experience, but I was in no hurry to go back. Greece, on the other hand, was our next planned location, and I was in a hurry to get there.

We left Casablanca in a chartered plane, bound for Athens. We were in midair, half way to our destination, when the co-pilot came hustling out of the cockpit. He was obviously agitated, a condition not calculated to reassure his passengers.

"We have just received a radio message," he told us. "We cannot land in Athens. The airport is closed. The borders are closed. There has been a *coup d'etat*. The military has taken over the government. Nobody can enter or leave the country."

This was devastating news. To me, it could mean more than mere delay. It could mean bankruptcy.

In anticipation of our Greek location, we had prepared scripts for the islands of Mykonos, Delos, Hydra, Crete, Santorini, and Rhodes. I had chartered an eighteen-ton inter-island vessel, the *Lina B.*, to serve as our hotel, our restaurant, and our transport, as we hopped from island to island. Fifty-six people would be on board. I had paid for the charter in advance and had provisioned the ship for a thirty-day itinerary. If I were to be denied the use of the ship, I would be in very large trouble. It would mean the loss of the large sum I had already paid for the charter and, even worse, it would mean that I wouldn't be able to meet my commitment to the network.

No play, no pay.

I had a quick huddle with Leon Chooluck, our location manager. First things first — let's get this damned plane on the ground. Leon got on the radio. Istanbul wouldn't take us because we had no Turkish visas. Ditto Lisbon. Biarritz turned us away because their parking space for aircraft was fully booked. Tangier likewise. It looked as though our plane was condemned to be the Flying Dutchman of the air.

The pilot consoled us. He said that if we circled until we were dangerously low on fuel, one of the airports would have to take us, lest we crash. Somehow I didn't find that alternative attractive. At the last minute, Lisbon relented and allowed us to land.

The next step was to get fifty-six people into a hotel. No hotel in Lisbon could take us. Leon kept trying, until we finally got lucky with a hotel in Estoril, a resort community a short distance out of Lisbon.

So far, so good. At least, we had a roof over our heads. The next order of business was to wrestle with the newly-established Greek revolutionary government to get our ship back. Meanwhile, we were hemorrhaging money.

After hours on the telephone, with the help of the American Embassy in Athens, I got through to one of the officials of the new government. He transferred my call to someone else, and he to a third official. I was passed from one bureaucrat to another like the ball in a soccer game. By the end of the day, I had reached the two-star general level.

I made an impassioned plea. I told him that the pictures I planned to make would be excellent public relations for Greece. They would show how beautiful the country was and how friendly the people were. All this would multiply the tourist trade, and since tourism was a major factor in the nation's economy, I had a potent argument.

The general told me to call back the next day. When I did, he told me the matter had been referred to his senior, a three-star general. "Call back tomorrow," he said.

What with hotel and per diem charges, crew salaries, equipment rental, a chartered plane sitting on the runway, and a host of etceteras, Leon figured that every day we were hung up in Portugal was costing me thirty thousand dollars. The cast and crew were far from unhappy. They were having a lovely time at my expense. They played baccarat in the casino. They found quaint little restaurants that served seafood freshly taken from the sea. They fished off the pier. They wandered around the countryside snapping pictures of colorfully-garbed natives and medieval castles. They fiddled while I burned.

When I finally got the three-star general on the phone, he promised to bring the matter up in a staff meeting and told me to call back tomorrow.

I said that I couldn't call back tomorrow, because I would be on the transatlantic phone all day, explaining to the American media how an American television company was being given the runaround by Greek army officers who had turned their lovely country into a prison. While I knew that this would have an unfortunate effect on the tourist trade, which was so important to the national economy, and I was sorry, I had an obligation to my countrymen. I had to tell it like it was.

The general asked me to hold the phone. I held the phone, twelve hundred escudos worth. When he came back on the line, he said that maybe something could be arranged, and that I should please call back tomorrow. Understandably, this sent chills down my spine. I told him I didn't think I could wait because the American media were hungry for my story. He promised that he would have definite news for me the next day, which could save me the expense of all those phone calls.

Okay. Put another thirty thousand dollars on my bill.

When I called back, I was instructed to fly my company to the island of Rhodes. The general would see that we were cleared to land there. We were to check into a designated hotel on the waterfront. Arrangements would have been made for our accommodation. We were to wait there for the *Lina B.* It would be delivered to us within forty-eight hours. Whoopee!

The hotel in Rhodes had a huge window looking out on the sunlit Aegean Sea on which nothing was afloat. Hour after hour, our marooned company stared out at an unbroken vista of sparkling sea, with only a carpet of azure water between us and the horizon.

Twilight came, followed by a moonlit, star-studded night. Still nothing. One by one, the weary watchers stretched, yawned, and took themselves off to bed, but I couldn't drag myself away from the window. It was under-standable. All they were losing was sleep. I was losing about a thousand dollars an hour.

I dozed through the night in a big leather armchair facing the window. The others rejoined me at sunrise and we resumed our vigil.

That morning, the harbor of Rhodes came alive with traffic, but none of it was ours. Three inter-island ships dropped anchor, and tenders plied the waters between them and the shore. They were unloading people. We later learned that the military junta that had engineered the coup d'état was sending prisoners to hastily-constructed prison camps on Crete and Rhodes.

Shortly after noon, we broke away from the window for lunch. Because I like to eat them separately, I was picking the black olives out of my Greek salad when the bell captain burst into the dining room and announced that there was something on the horizon. We rushed out. The something was a smudge of smoke, and as we watched, it grew into the superstructure of a ship. Then the hull came into view, and there she was, our *Lina B*. She was to be our home for the next month.

Our scheduled work on the island of Rhodes went smoothly. It was a lovely place to work. The south shore of the island is fringed with beaches carpeted with snow white sand, soft as powder. There is an acropolis, topped by the ruins of a two-thousand-year-old temple.

We got a lot of good stuff on the island of Rhodes. The historic ruins, silhouetted against cloudless skies, made good pictures. The capital city is a treasure chest of memories of the Crusaders. They paved streets and built fortresses that are still intact.

When it came time for us to move on, the *Lina B.* was ready. Life on board the ship was pleasant. Frankie and I had the captain's cabin, right behind the wheel house. Each morning, I leaned over the bow rail and shouted, "Sail on, and on," just to feel what it was like to be Christopher Columbus. There were only fifty-six of us spread out in a ship that could accommodate eighty-six. The cast and crew were housed in spacious quarters.

Cosby had a large cabin near the stern, to which he would repair for a nap right after lunch. One afternoon, Mort Fine watched the chef sorting a mess of freshly-caught fish. Still alive, they were flapping vigorously on the deck. Struck by an evil thought, Mort borrowed several of the fish and took them to the door of the cabin in which Cosby was napping. He tossed them over the transom, yelling, "The ship is sinking! Everybody on deck!" Cosby came awake, saw live fish flap-flap-flapping on his cabin floor, and came out of there like a scorched-ass rabbit!

We became accustomed to Greek food and drink during the weeks spent aboard the *Lina B.* Black olives, feta cheese, and spitted lamb are easy to like, but *retsina* is an acquired taste. It is a variety of Greek wine that has been matured in a cask lined with tar, and it tastes like a freshly-laid macadam road smells. It dates back many centuries, to the time when wine was shipped from port to port in huge jugs.

Believe it or not, if you try hard enough, you can get to like it.

Ouzo is easier to take to. It is a powerful, aniseflavored kind of liqueur. It is served by the carafe, not by the glass. The Greeks play a game in which you empty the carafe, and then try to stand up from your chair.

The ship took us to fascinating places. Nowadays, everybody knows about Mykonos, but when we were there it was a beautiful, sleepy, undiscovered island. The town was, as it is now, a gleaming white gem. A friendly pelican paraded up and down along the waterfront, cadging scraps from the diners in the sidewalk cafes. Fishermen pounded octopi to tenderness on the boards of the quay. Sponge divers dried their harvest in the sun.

Holding a stopwatch, I refereed a breath-holding contest between two sponge divers. The winner held his breath for three minutes and twenty-seven seconds. We caught a lot of the wonderful local color on film. It was why I had been eager to get out of the studios.

Crete was interesting in a way different from any of the other Islands. Knossos, the capital city of the Minoan civilization, dating back as far as 3000 B.C., is built close to the ruins of ancient royal palaces. The corridors of the well-preserved palaces are lined with frescoes depicting the battles, sports, religious practices, and customs of the ancient Cretan people. Thousands of years ago, they practiced a form of bullfighting, but instead of controlling the bull with cape and muleta, their bullfighters were trained to somersault over the back of the charging bull. Some fun, eh?

Delos is little changed from the pre-Christian days. Most of the ancient dwellings on the island are roofless, but the Mediterranean climate has been kind to the mosaics and frescoes. When we were there in 1969, we were allowed to roam freely around the island, exploring the ruins. If the people who govern Greece have any sense, they will have established rules to protect their ancient heritage from the kind of damage that unrestricted tourism can inflict.

The island of Santorini, or Thera, as it was called, is what remains of an extinct volcano. At any rate, everybody hopes it is extinct. At one time, many centuries ago, it was very much alive. It erupted, blew away its southern rim, and the sea rushed in to fill the void and quench the flames. The sea has filled the bottomless crater, turning it into a fine harbor.

When the traveler comes ashore, he lands on a ledge cut into the wall of the crater. The town is high above the sea, on the rim of the volcano. If you're in good shape, you can trudge up to it by way of a winding road that clings to the wall of the enormous pit; or you can give one of the ever-present muleteers a few coins, and ride his patient, plodding animal to the top. In either case, you will be rewarded by a wonderful view. Far below you is a sapphire sea nestled in a perfect circle formed by the embracing arms of the black-lava crater walls. White cruise ships ride serenely on the gentle swells.

Fuad had appropriated a restaurant on the rim. He was a fine chef, with a special talent for shish kebab. Each evening, we ate and drank, and watched the sun sink into the darkening sea. It was a tough way of life, but we bore it uncomplainingly.

Photographing the Greek islands proved to be a frustrating experience. No two islands are alike and each has its own character. There was so much to capture on film and so little time in which to do it.

Athens would be just another city if it weren't for the Acropolis. Everybody has seen pictures of the Parthenon, but pictures can't even suggest the awe you feel when you actually stand in front of the majestic structure that crowns the Acropolis. When we were there, we were unrestricted, free to scramble over the place, to dig up souvenirs, or even to scratch our names in the marble, God forbid. Since then, many areas have been put off limits, lest exploding tourism do what the centuries couldn't.

The relics of Greece's history are breathtaking. The simple elegance of their architecture, dating back to pre-Christian days, has never been equaled. And their sculpture!

Long before the artists of the Christian world were struggling to understand the elements of composition and per-
spective, the Greeks were carving marble into
representations of the human body that were not to be
matched until the appearance of Michelangelo. They were
carving history into the friezes of their temples — friezes of
such beauty and importance that when Lord Elgin looted the
marble frieze that Phidias had carved for the Parthenon, it
caused an international brouhaha that continues till this day.

In Greece, we captured ghosts of the past on film
every day. As we got deeper into our schedule, I was
intrigued by a minor mystery, which resolved itself one night
on top of Mount Attavynos, in a restaurant overlooking the
capital city.

At that time, many Greek restaurants had an intriguing custom, which has since been curtailed by unimagina-
tive legislation. Those restaurants featured bouzouki music,
and when the mandolin-like instruments really got to twang-
ing, men rose up from their tables and made their way to the
dance floor to go into the stately, measured cadences of
Greek dancing. Never women. Always men.

If the diners liked what they saw, they threw table
plates into the air, to shatter on the dance floor. A charge for
the plates would appear on their bills.

Frankie and I were having dinner in the restaurant on
Mount Attavynos when I spotted Dimi lurking at the bar.
Dimi, or Demetrios, a burly ex-wrestler, had a shiny bald
head and an unpronounceable last name, full of o's and u's.

Leon had signed him on to push or haul heavy things
as needed, but Dimi aspired to more than that.

Soon after Leon employed him, Dimi came to me, and
said, "You put me in picture. Yes?"

I told him I couldn't think of any way we could use
him in front of the camera.

"Is plenty ways," he told me. "I do plenty things."

I dismissed him with a vague promise to think about it. In the following days, I sensed his presence near me much of the time. Now, he was here watching my wife and me as we had dinner. It was disconcerting. Why was he shadowing me? What did he plan? I soon saw.

As the music heated up, Dimi got up from his stool by the bar and made his way to the dance floor. Raising his arms, he picked up the tempo of the music and moved into the rhythms of the dance. With his bulk and his shining, bald head he made an arresting spectacle as he performed the traditional movements with surprising grace.

An appreciative diner hurled a plate. Like a lizard's tongue snatching a fly in mid-flight, Dimi's hand flashed out, picked the plate out of the air, and with every movement timed to the rhythm of the dance, smashed the plate on his shiny, bald head!

Well, that started it!

Soon, the air was filled with flying plates, and Dimi's skull was rattling like a bongo drum.

It was something to behold!

The next day Dimi got his wish. We rewrote a street scene to play in a restaurant, and Dimi was its centerpiece.

Greece was a fine location. No previous film company had done the islands as completely as we had. Our accomplishments in Greece whetted my appetite for more exotic locations to conquer.

How about China?

Or the Soviet Union?

For some time, I had been carrying on correspondence with the cultural attachés of the Russian and Chinese embassies. I drooled over the idea of shooting in China. There is no more glamorous and exciting setting for picture making than the Forbidden City in Beijing, as director Bernardo Bertolucci demonstrated when he made the Academy-Award-winner, *The Last Emperor.*

The Great Wall, the only man-made structure on earth that can be seen from the moon, had been seen only in travelogues, never on entertainment TV. What a coup if I could get permission to shoot there!

As it turned out, getting permission wasn't difficult. The Chinese officials were eager to open their country to tourism and, consequently, my proposal interested them.

I asked if I could shoot on the Great Wall.

Certainly, they said.

The Forbidden City?

Of course.

The Stone Forest, the excavations at Xiang, the Kweilin Valley?

Yes, yes, and yes.

There was one non-negotiable stipulation. I could shoot as much film as I wished in China, but I couldn't ship it back to America until after the Chinese officials had screened it. This meant that it would have to be processed in China.

I researched the Chinese film processing facilities. As I had feared, they were primitive. The product they turned out was grainy and lacking in contrast. The colors were muddy. Film processed in China would not have met the networks' broadcast quality standards.

I suggested to the Chinese officials that they could have a designated representative in the United States view the film, after I had it processed in our laboratories.

They said "No Dice," or the Chinese equivalent. They had to see it before I shipped it. Since that was an unacceptable condition, I said goodbye to the Forbidden City, which was not to delight American audiences until a more enlightened administration modified the rules, fifteen years later.

The Soviets were a different story. They had fine laboratories, in some respects more advanced than ours. Their motion picture studios were also more advanced than most of ours, because they had been built later and weren't burdened with obsolescent equipment. They were, on the whole, more "state of the art" than our comparable facilities.

Frankie and I took ourselves off to Moscow, armed with letters of introduction. The Soviet Film Agency and related departments knew all about me. They knew about *I Spy*. Since the series was based on espionage, and since the natural opponents for our guys in the spy business were guys from the other side of the Iron Curtain — from Russia or its satellites — *I Spy* had been thoroughly scouted by the various Soviet information services. They didn't like it. I didn't blame them. Their guys were always the losers.

I proposed that the Soviet filmmakers join me in developing stories that emphasized the benefits of cooperation between the great powers, and soft-pedaled the rivalries. After all, we shared a common goal — survival — and our survival, the survival of the whole human race, depended on peace.

I wanted to do stories that made it clear that it was in our common interest to link hands in the fight against terrorism, against nuclear proliferation, and against provocation.

They applauded my proposal, and promised that I could expect full cooperation. Naturally, there would be certain conditions. They would have to have collaborative rights in plot development. I considered that a reasonable condition. They wanted to appoint two writers to work with my writers, but they agreed that the right of final approval of the script and its contents would rest with me. They stipulated that we were to use Russian labor in all categories, except cast, director, producer, and department heads — head cameraman, head electrician, etc. I foresaw difficulty there. My department heads would want to work with their own people. I was sure some compromise could be worked out. The stipulation didn't seem to be a deal-breaker, but I wanted a little time to think about it.

While all this had been going on, Frankie and I had been seizing every opportunity for sightseeing. A guide and a car and driver had been assigned to us. Since the meetings and negotiations had been spread over a period of several weeks, we had found plenty of time to behave like tourists.

We spent days in the incredible Pushkin Museum in Moscow. We made a three-day side trip to Leningrad, and were overwhelmed by the even more incredible Hermitage Museum there.

There simply aren't adequate adjectives with which to describe the treasures that the Czarist regime and its aristocrats had accumulated, only to have them confiscated by the revolutionary government: precious Fabergé eggs, antique furniture, paintings by the thousands — Primitives, Old Masters, Cubists, Impressionists. The nobles of the last Czar's court were particularly fond of the French Impressionists, with whom they were contemporary. Because they collected them avidly, the Pushkin and the Hermitage have the largest and finest collection of that genre to be found anywhere in the world.

Our guide, Sonya, was a comfortable, multi-lingual, middle-aged lady. In a country where very few people speak English, she was indispensable.

Our hotel accommodations were surprisingly lush for such a Spartan country. We had a big, well-furnished suite in the Rusya Hotel, overlooking St. Basil's Cathedral and Red Square. Right beneath our window was Lenin's Tomb, with its perpetual line of worshippers, stretching away for hundreds of yards, come to view his marvelously preserved body.

One night, in the privacy of our suite, Frankie and I were discussing the possibility of visiting the town of

Bershad, in the Ukraine. I had been told that my grandparents, on my father's side, had emigrated from that village. They had, in fact, drawn their surname from the name of the village. We decided that we would enquire about the possibility of visiting it.

The next morning, when we met Sonya, she greeted us saying, "I asked about visiting the village in the Ukraine, and the officials tell me that it will take three weeks to arrange the permits. You are scheduled to leave before that, so I'm afraid your visit there will have to wait until the next time you come to Russia."

We hadn't mentioned our desire to visit the village to her. We hadn't mentioned it to anyone. The only place it had been mentioned was in our suite.

What conclusion was I to draw?

From then on, we were very careful about what we talked about in our suite.

As days passed, we became increasingly aware of a characteristic of the communist system. Working people below the level of officialdom were, on the whole, unmotivated. Nobody worked very hard. Why knock yourself out? You weren't going anywhere, and nobody was going to fire you.

Service in the hotels and restaurants was lousy. It took from two to three hours to get dinner served. I could imagine the state of Leon Chooluck's nerves while his company had two- or three-hour lunches. An unwelcome question entered my thinking, and demanded an answer.

I took a typical *I Spy* script to the studio production office, and asked the department head to break it down for me and schedule it. Two days later, I got his answer. He had scheduled it for nineteen days. In Greece, we had filmed such a script in eight.

Well, it had seemed like a good idea at the time.

Regretfully, I said goodbye to Russia.

Making pictures on foreign locations is difficult, but the result, what you can finally put on the screen, supports my belief that the end justifies the means.

The first two years of *I Spy* had been a triumph. The Cosby-Culp team had immediate acceptance. Cosby had been a show business phenomenon, winning Emmy awards three years in row. The series had won all sort of awards, Emmies, Golden Globes, and Critics' Awards. It had consistently won its time spot — ten o'clock on Wednesday night — over the competing networks. It was so strong that NBC decided to use it, in its upcoming third season, to bolster their weak Monday night lineup.

They proposed to have it follow a new Thomas--Spelling anthology series, and opposite a nondescript show on ABC and a girl comic on CBS. I fought the move. We were comfortable where we were. If it's not broke, don't fix it. I was overruled. They assured me we would do very well in the new spot — the Thomas-Spelling show would be a strong lead-in, and we'd murder the girl comic. The Thomas--Spelling anthology bombed, leaving us with no lead-in; the girl comic turned out to be Carol Burnett.

I Spy slid from near the top of the ratings list to a place in the bottom half.

As its third year came to a close, Mort Werner and Herb Schlosser asked for a meeting with me to discuss the future of *I Spy*. They had a problem, which they dumped in my lap.

NBC was contractually obligated to put a new one-hour show on the air for me. I had submitted several ideas, and they had selected an hour-mystery series, starring a young Italian actor, Enzo Cerusico, whom I had used with great success when I was shooting in Rome. He was sort of an Italian version of Maurice Chevalier. I proposed to pair him with James Whitmore, as a crime-solving team.

Whitmore was to be the brains of the combination, Cerusico was to be the legs.

There was nothing startlingly new about the idea, but then there's nothing new about flour, eggs, and butter. However, they can be combined, and recombined, into an enormous variety of eatables. Similarly, there are a limited number of ingredients with which to make an entertainment package — comedy, tragedy, sex, danger, romance — but they can be remixed in unlimited combinations. It's up to the chef who is cooking up the dish to flavor it differently.

We have been using those same ingredients since the first cave man, sitting in a ring around the fire, entertained his fellow Neanderthals with a dramatized tale of how he pursued, caught, and killed a mastodon — conveying to his audience the excitement of the chase, and the drama of the slaughter.

My Friend Tony, the show the network was committed to air, was a pleasant combination of Cerusico's Italian charm and Whitmore's Yankee stability, with a dash of danger, a soupçon of mystery, and a pinch of humor. Everybody liked the idea, but the network claimed that there was no room for it in the schedule. They said there was only a single unassigned time spot for the upcoming season. If I insisted that they honor their contractual commitment to *Tony*, *I Spy* would have to be dropped. They said it was up to me.

It was a difficult decision to make. *Tony* was far from a sure thing. It was aimed at the young audience, with whom Cerusico's impish charm was most likely to score, and unless it got an appropriate time spot it wasn't going to last long. On the other hand, *I Spy* was a pretty sure bet to continue for at least a couple of seasons, if I accepted its renewal in place of *Tony*. However, in my opinion, it would limp through those seasons, losing much of its syndication value.

The unique economics of television was a dominant consideration in the decision I was being asked to make.

Although licensing fees had risen astronomically since we were paid thirty thousand an episode for *The Danny Thomas Show*, a TV packager seldom made a profit on the network run of his show. Even today, very few shows turn a profit in their first run, because production costs have a miraculous ability to keep pace with, or a little ahead of, increased income.

If the show's owner is to make anything more than his per-episode production fee, it will come from reruns and syndication — that is, if the show has had healthy ratings. A low-rated show has little rerun value. I was getting two hundred thousand per episode for *I Spy*, but it wasn't enough. *I Spy* had been lavishly produced. It had been running a deficit with each episode, and I was deeply in the red. I figured to recoup with syndication sales, but since it had been knocked down in the ratings, its rerun value had been seriously impaired. If it was kept in its present time spot, ratings could only get worse, and so would my chances of getting even.

As a point of interest, Bill Cosby's deal for a seventh season of *The Cosby Show* called for two million dollars per half-hour episode! Granted that this was a special case, but these days, run-of-the-mill half-hour shows are budgeted at six or seven hundred thousand per episode. Has everybody gone crazy?

When Werner couldn't promise to return *I Spy* to its Wednesday time period, I opted to let it go, in favor of *My Friend Tony*.

It was the end of a marvelous adventure.

So, *I Spy* came off the air and *My Friend Tony* went on, but not for long. It seems that in making the decision to pull *I Spy*, I had stepped on some important toes.

The network executive (So help me, I've forgotten the bastard's name. Talk about a Freudian block!) had falsely claimed a shortage of time slots to make me forgo my contractual right to put a second hour on NBC, because in his opinion, that represented too many eggs in one basket. He didn't think I'd give up *I Spy* in favor of *My Friend Tony*, but when I trumped his ace by doing so, he figured he'd fix me.

He jockeyed his schedule around, and *My Friend Tony* wound up at ten p.m. Sunday night. We'll never know if *Tony* could have been a successful show, because the adolescent audience, for which it had been designed, is simply not available at ten p.m., Sunday night. *My Friend Tony* was canceled at the end of its first year.

When the decision to cancel *I Spy* was announced in the press, Bill Cosby called me, hoping I'd say it wasn't true. He wanted it to keep going, even though it meant major financial sacrifices for him. His career was booming, and night clubs were paying him many times the meager salary he was getting from me for *I Spy*. If he continued to do the show, he would have to pass up many lucrative engagements. It didn't make good business sense for him, but Cosby is afflicted with a serious case of loyalty, and he wanted to continue working with the people to whom he had become attached.

We've remained friends through the years.

fourteen

Changes

I've worked in many departments of the entertainment business. Directing yields great creative satisfaction, producing-packaging pays the most money, but acting provides the most ego gratification. It rewards with more than money. It yields the flattery of public recognition and approval. It was to feed my unsated appetite for acting that I accepted Cosby's invitation to do a guest spot on the spectacularly successful *Bill Cosby Show*. Boy! was my ego massaged!

Cosby sent a stretch limousine to pick me up at my Manhattan hotel. When I arrived at the entrance to his studio, in the Flatbush section of Brooklyn, I stepped onto a red carpet, specially provided for the occasion. I was embraced by Jay Sandrich, Cosby's director, whom I had started as a director way back in the days of *The Danny Thomas Show*.

He said, "Come on. Bill had your dressing room specially prepared. He wants you to be comfortable. He really went all out. Wait until you see it."

We entered the studio, and Jay led me down a corridor, stopping in front of a door with a brass plate on it. My name was engraved on the plate. Not stamped on. *Engraved*. Wow! Jay threw open the door.

Cobwebs drooled from the ceiling of the dismally dark cubicle. A broken chair leaned forlornly against the wall. A veritable herd of rats scurried about on the litter-covered floor.

Yes, indeed! Cosby had gone all out to make me feel at home!

Then Jay led me to my real dressing room. While it didn't have an engraved nameplate on the door, it had been prepared with thoughtful care, furnished with comfortable chairs, a sofa, a TV set, a tape player, a refrigerator, and a well-stocked bar.

It sure wasn't like that when I made my living acting.

All of television is different and the changes had started with the defection of the sponsors.

When I first got into television, the radio-originated role of the sponsor had prevailed. The network was merely a rental facility, a showcase in which the sponsor chose to display his series. When a sponsor bought a show, he shopped around for a time spot and a network. He placed the show in the spot he had chosen, and he kept it on the air as long as it pleased him, whether or not the network liked it. The show became identified with the sponsor's product.

As television audiences grew, so did the cost of television advertising. It got to a point where it consumed too much of the sponsor's advertising budget, at the expense of other media. Full sponsorship became a luxury that few could afford. Guided by their advertising agencies, the sponsors gradually adopted a policy called "the magazine concept." Instead of buying total sponsorship of a single show, they bought commercial minutes on several, as one might buy pages of advertising in different magazines.

By relinquishing sponsorship, they also relinquished control. Their abdication left a vacuum which network personnel rushed in to fill. It had been the custom for a TV packager to take his pilot to New York and screen it for dozens of potential buyers. When the sponsors retreated, the market for new projects was reduced to three customers — the networks. This reduction in their potential markets was a severe financial blow to the packagers of TV entertainment, but the creative damage was much worse.

The media buyer for a large company might buy a show because his kids liked it, or because he had always thought Milton Berle was funny. The networks bought a show because it tested in the upper twenty percentile of electronically-recorded audience response. The personal response was replaced by a computer-generated response.

The procedure went like this, and perhaps still does: The network ran your pilot in an auditorium, called a "preview house." There each seat was fitted with a hand-operated dial connected to a central computer. The audience was instructed to move the dial forward or backward, in accordance with the degree of pleasure they were experiencing as they watched your pilot. No kidding!

It should have been obvious that this routine disregarded several axioms of the entertainment trade. An audience should be relaxed and receptive, if you hope to entertain them. They shouldn't be asking themselves, "How much do I really like this scene? Should I give it a seven or an eight on a scale of ten?"

Before an audience can get involved in a scene, they must care about the characters in it. Unless the character is Lucille Ball, Bob Hope, or a similar icon, such identification does not occur in the first minutes of a half-hour pilot. Yet an investment of months of time and large sums of money can be knocked out of the box because "it didn't test well."

All in the Family didn't test well. Neither did *The Dick Van Dyke Show*. *M*A*S*H* didn't test well, nor did *Andy Griffith*. The more multi-dimensional the characters in a piece are, the longer it takes the audience to get to know them and identify with them. But once a show gets this identification, it can run forever. Witness the daytime soap operas. In the trade they say such shows "have legs."

It was when the sponsors dropped control of television into the networks' laps that the obsession with ratings began. The bigger the numbers, the more could be charged for each commercial minute. Sponsors kept their shows alive as long they liked them; networks stayed with a show as long as its ratings were high.

The changes that were occurring in broadcasting weren't all due to gut feelings being replaced by the computer. Many of them were due to accountants, lawyers, and corporate raiders replacing showmen. Irving Berlin said it, "There are no people like show people," and indeed there aren't. They don't know from graphs, spread sheets or percentiles, but they know how to work an audience like a matador knows how to work a bull.

When the sponsors backed out, the networks stepped in with program executives heavy on theory and light on experience.

Shortly before Jack Benny's demise, I did one of my frequent guest spots with him. I was deeply involved in television production at that time, but whenever Jack's writers asked me to appear as "The Tout," the role they had created for me, I hastened to oblige.

After one broadcast, Jack told me he had an idea for a television series, and since that was my line of work, he wanted my opinion. The concept dealt with the romance between a very liberated young woman and a young Italian who was a male chauvinist by heritage, having been brought up in a traditional Italian household, where papa was the unchallenged boss. In spite of their ideological differences, they fall deeply in love, and the comedy derives from the wealth of conflict inherent in the situation.

It was a pretty good idea, and I told him so. He said that if I liked it, I could have it. I protested. He insisted that he'd just been fooling around with a notion and he wasn't interested in taking it any further.

"Ideas are cheap," I told him. "They grow on every tree. It's the people who are going to carry out the idea that are important. If I were to go to the network and say, 'Jack

Benny came up with a good idea for a series and he agreed to be an executive consultant on it,' I'd have their attention."

After more persuasion, Jack agreed to go at least that far with me. The Morris office made an appointment for us at NBC, where we met with the newly-installed West Coast head of programming and his multitude of assistants.

After the obligatory coffee ritual, he said, "I hear you've got something for us, Jack."

Jack outlined his idea, and, being Jack Benny, he made it sound very good. When he finished there was brief silence while the acolytes looked around to see who was going to stick his neck out first.

The head man spoke. "I think you've got something there, Jack," he said. "I don't think it can work the way you told it, but I can tell you how to fix it."

I went into shock, but Jack never missed a beat.

"I'd love to hear you tell me how to fix it," he said, "but I've got an appointment with my dentist for some root canal work. I've been looking forward to it for weeks, so if you'll excuse me...." and he made a majestic exit.

Such experiences with the new breed were not unique. Hans Conried, a marvelously versatile actor, agreed to an interview with a brand new producer. The young man didn't bother to take his sneakered feet off his desk when Hans entered his office.

The newly-anointed producer said to him, "Well, Mr. Conried. Tell me what you've done."

To which Hans replied, "You first."

The networks have adopted the motto "Think Young!" Experience, because it is associated with age, has become an employment liabilty. Writers, directors, and producers who are over thirty find it hard to get work.

But experience *is* important. In fact, there are few areas of human activity in which experience is more important than in the entertainment business.

I'd learned that first-hand, when Sol Bury, my friend from *Having Wonderful Time*, had introduced me to the back-stage life of the world of burlesque, the home of down-to-earth, elementary showmanship based on sex, comedy, and spectacle — the world of strippers, comics, straight men, and line girls. Practicing pragmatists, all of them. If the bit works, keep it in. If it doesn't work, throw it out.

Every stripper tried different routines until she found the one that worked for her. There were shy strippers and bold strippers, slow strippers and fast strippers; strippers who worked with fans and strippers who worked with balloons, strippers who worked with feathers and strippers who worked with snakes.

All the burlesque comics had trunks full of sketch material. Literally, trunks full. The material was never copyrighted. It was considered common property. All around the circuit, from coast to coast, such sketches as "Slowly I Turned," "Niagara Falls," and "The Invisible Bartender" were standard. When a comic opened in a new house, he asked the manager for the straight man or talking woman he needed for his sketches. They didn't need any rehearsal. Everybody knew the material.

This was basic, elementary show biz, the kind I understood. I didn't understand the kind of show business television had become. It was time to retire.

"Show Business" is an awkward term, but how else do you designate the various forms of entertainment — theatre, movies, television, variety, ballet, opera? Whatever you choose to call it, I can't think of a more exciting, gratifying, frustrating, rewarding, aggravating, fulfilling form of work. It is so all-consuming that when those of us who have spent most of a lifetime in it come to the point of retirement, we have a dilemma that doesn't exist for most others.

What to do?

Other retiring professionals may look forward to the pursuit of hobbies — golf, gardening, stamp collecting — but our profession is our hobby. I don't know anyone in show business who wouldn't rather be on a stage than on a golf course. And how can you compare landing a twenty-pound striped bass to getting a ten-second laugh from a studio audience?

At various times in the not-so-distant past, I have accepted invitations to lecture at universities. I conducted a couple of seminars at my alma mater, Syracuse University, at UCLA, Cal State, USC, and others. I thought I would enjoy helping young people get a start in show business. It didn't turn out that way. Instead of liking the lecturing experience, I was depressed by it. Very early on, it became apparent that while the eager young people I was addressing were full of energy, ambition, and hope, they were not full of talent. Instead of helping them to make it in the entertainment trades, I was luring them on to frustration, disappointment, and failure.

The excitement and glamour of show business attract young people in search of a career like syrup attracts flies. Many of them, in fact most of them, don't belong. Talent is a rare thing, and if there is one thing you should have if you're going into show business, it's talent. You don't have to be handsome — look at Woody Allen. You don't have to be beautiful — look at Roseanne. But you damned well better be talented.

All their young lives, my two kids, Andrea and Steve, were exposed to the glamour and appeal of show business. Frankie and I watched them through childhood and adolescence, looking for some sign of those characteristics that would indicate they might want to follow where I had led. No way!

Steve had his eyes set on a career in business, Andrea was to become a psychiatric social worker. They were both fortunate in that they wound up doing things they enjoyed, things they did well. That's the secret of a successful career, whether it be in show business, law, medicine, or prostitution.

As for me, the fear of retirement turned out to be unjustified. To this day, I get an occasional request to do a guest spot as an actor. If I like the show and the material, I'm eager to do it. It keeps my acting muscles from atrophying. Now that I've gained some understanding of word processing, I can always spend a couple of hours at the computer, pounding out random thoughts, such as these. I am on the board of directors of the Permanent Charities Committee, the Motion Picture and Television Home, the Directors Guild of America. I am the Secretary-Treasurer of the Guild, as well as Chairman of the Building Committee and a founder and member of the Guild's Special Projects Committee. I lead seminars around the country. I average four committee or board meetings a week. I play golf in the low nineties — on rare occasions in the high eighties. Last year, off the coast of Cabo San Lucas, I caught an eighty-eight-pound rooster fish — a world record.

If this be retirement, I'm making the best of it.

In April of 1993, when I put the dust cover on my word processor and stacked the white pages in an old stationery box, I believed I was through with these memoirs. I had told about more than half-century of involvement in the theatre, movies, radio, and television. That pretty well covers it, I thought. I didn't know that I was about to get into what was, for me, a strange new form of show business — sucked in by my old buddy, Bill Cosby.

He called me one day and said that he had been nursing a long-standing yen to recapture the fun and adventure of making *I Spy*, and now that he was through with his series he was free to indulge himself. CBS was eager to give him a commitment, so I was to get off my duff and put together something bright and charming for him and his old sidekick, Bob Culp. Scott and Kelly were to ride again!

The idea did not enchant me. I am not particularly ambitious or acquisitive, I had just gotten my golf handicap down to twenty, and the blue marlin were running off Cabo San Lucas. But Bill is persuasive.

I came up with the idea of a second generation of aspiring spies: Scott's daughter and Kelly's son. I accepted an invitation to pitch the premise to the network executives in charge of movies at CBS. They liked it. I said, "I have just the right guy in mind to do the script. He's an Oscar winner. He has a flair for bright dialogue, and he can handle the tough mix of comedy and action."

"Who have you got in mind?"

I told them.

"He's not acceptable."

"Come again?"

"He's not on our list of acceptable writers."

"I'm sure I'm not on your list either," I said. And I walked out.

Turmoil in the offices of the William Morris Agency! "You don't do that to CBS," I was told. "If you behave like that you can kill the deal!" was spoken with intonations of horror that would have been appropriate if we had been discussing killing the president.

"Why? If they're going to tell me who I can and can't use, why do they need me? Let them do it. I'll give them the premise. Count me out."

Cosby got on the phone. I agreed to another meeting with the network people to see if we could find an area for compromise. I showed up on time, defiantly wearing sneakers and without a necktie. After the obligatory coffee and small talk preliminaries, the woman in charge called the meeting to order. "We don't want you to think that we're being arbitrary. We're open to any reasonable compromise. Now, here's a list of writers we would find acceptable."

"I don't pick my writers off a list," I told them. "See you later!" And I was out of there.

More turmoil. More phone calls. More arm twisting. I agreed to a third meeting.

This time, they were ready for me. I had the feeling that everybody in the room had been briefed. "This guy is crazy. Handle him with care."

"Okay. We're reasonable people. We'll give your guy a shot at it. Have him submit an outline."

Under the circumstances, this was as much of a victory as I could have hoped for. I called up my guy. "Frank," I said, "you're set. Have your agent call CBS and set your deal."

"Gosh, Shel, I don't know. I've been thinking about it. If they're so negative before I even get started, it's going to be a ball-breaker. Who needs it? Count me out."

The next morning I went back to CBS and said to the woman in charge, "May I see that list?" My new education in dealing with the networks was under way. I had to learn a new set of rules.

Network executives have always had the right of approval of the central elements on a project: director, writer, principal cast members, composer. Now it quickly becomes apparent that this "right of approval" is, in fact, the right of selection, since, if they keep turning down the people the producer wants, sooner or later he's going to come to the name they had in mind from the beginning. Nice, huh?

The Directors Guild has a contract with the producers stipulating that the director shall have the right to participate in the selection of cast members and in the development and revision of the script. Then how come these rights have become virtually meaningless? Because, I am told, the network is the buyer, and as the buyer they are free to say, "This is what we want."

It must be understood that I had been away from the trade for more than twenty years. When I was in harness, responsible for multiple shows at the top of the Nielsen ratings and bolstered by the backing of such powerful sponsors as General Foods and Procter & Gamble, I had enjoyed complete autonomy. Now I had a bridle jammed in my mouth and I didn't like the feel of it.

I checked out several of the writers acceptable to the network people. I called producers they had worked for. I had their agents submit sample scripts, and I wound up with a talented guy named Michael Norell. Together we steered the script through the hazards of first and second draft. It wasn't easy.

After submitting the second draft, we received a seven page memo from CBS. The first two pages of the communiqué cover philosophy of drama in two sections:

1) Scott and Kelly/Character Relationship. This portion begins: "Our audience has considerable expectations of these men — Scott and Kelly were the first fully grown, masculine team of their era. They (sic) created the modern 'Buddy Movie' concept. They were funniest when the situation was bleakest. Use this irony more in our script......Let's not sell our guys short. They can be silly, over-concerned and even over-the-hill. But where is their genuine growth? Where is that moment between them? How has the world changed for them? There is no triumph finally. No tragedy. No gain. No loss, no coming together, not in any meaningful sense."

I replied to this that I did not understand what was meant by "their genuine growth." What growth? Physical? Intellectual? Financial? Political?

Who cares how the world has changed for them?

And what is meant by "no tragedy, no pain, no coming together."

In fact, I asked, "What the hell does the whole paragraph mean?"

2) Plot/Jeopardy/High Stakes. This starts: "Though we seem to approach it, we never feel a sense of <u>real</u> danger, <u>real</u> jeopardy."

The writer of the memo either never saw any of the original *I Spys*, or did not appreciate their scrupulously maintained tone. Not only was the series basically tongue-in-cheek, but the jeopardy to which our principals were exposed always had to take into account that our audience knew that Scott and Kelly would be alive next week.

The remainder of the CBS memo consisted of copious "page notes" that critiqued character relationships, dialogue, incident, motivations, and even outlined a whole new final scene.

My reply concluded "....though I have been assured by my associates that network requests are usually negotiable, I must make it plain that, in defense of a valuable property, my position is not."

I was never noted for diplomacy.

After a series of such confrontations, the final draft of the script was approved and I got a green light to go into production. Then came the matter of selecting a director. I knew just what I wanted from whoever was to direct the piece. He would start with a nice tight script and a fine cast. His principal job would be to maintain a delicate balance between comedy and credibility.

If credibility is not a consideration, you can go all out — like the 007 pictures or *Get Smart* — and have a lot of fun, and that's all right. Or, if humor is not a factor, you can make total credibility your goal — à la John le Carre — and come out with a gripping film. But, if you want a reasonable level of credibility and a discreet seasoning of comedy, you need a director with a high level of taste in both those areas.

Such taste is not acquired fresh out of a class in directing. It comes from years of trying your stuff out on an audience. I submitted to the network the name of a director who had such experience. He was turned down without explanation. Likewise, my second choice.

No matter how they danced around the subject, it was clear that both of the directors I suggested were rejected by the network because they were too old.

It is an inescapable fact that, for some years, all three networks have been obsessed with the pursuit of a young audience. To that end, and to repeat myself, they have been favoring youth over experience in the selection of writers, directors, and other key personnel.

That was the ground on which I chose to attack. Threatening to take my complaint to the federal level, I was prepared to prove, with an endless array of eager witnesses, that the networks were practicing age discrimination. Like any other bully, the networks will back away from a bare-knuckle fight. I got a director of my choice.

And so it went.

There were countless confrontations when it came to casting. I won some and lost some. Several decades ago, I would have enjoyed the challenge of these face-offs. Now I dreaded them. It got to be all too easy to say "The hell with it." But whenever I did, I regretted it later.

Take the matter of casting an actor for the part of Baroodi, the heavy in our picture. There is a scene in which Scott and Kelly force Baroodi out into the crowded lobby of a Viennese hotel, naked! The actor I wanted for the part is talented, experienced, and fat. I cherished the idea of a naked fat man scrambling around a crowded hotel lobby! The network said no. We were already in production. Days went by as I wrestled with the network people. We got closer and closer to the time when I had to release Cosby. Finally, I said, "The hell with it." I settled for a talented thin actor.

The scene would have been funnier with a fat actor.

With it all, the picture came out well. My latest encounter with the networks is over, but a new phase is about to begin. I think they are doing a grave disservice to a medium that has treated me well, and I'm going to try to do something about it.

Like I said, my golf handicap is down and the blue marlin are running, but I still have time on my hands.

Sound the trumpets! Beat the drums! Where is the valet with my armor?

Wish me luck.

Broadway Theatre

Actor

1934: *Hotel Alimony*	1937: *Having Wonderful Time*
1935: *Fly Away Home*	1937: *Siege*
1937: *Three Men on a Horse*	1938: *Kiss the Boys Goodbye*
(road)	1939: *Margin for Error* (road)

Radio (Selected credits)

Actor

Beginning in:

    1941: (NBC): *Duffy's Tavern*

"   1943 (CBS): *The Judy Canova Show*
       role: Joe Crunchmiller, the taxi driver.

"   1945 (CBS): *Maisie* (starring Ann Sothern)

"   1945 (NBC): *Meet Me at Parky's*
       role: Orville Sharp

"   1946 (CBS): *The Jack Benny Show*
       role: The Tout

"   1946 (NBC): *The Phil Harris Show* (*The Fitch
       Bandwagon*) role: Grogan

Occasional episodes:

    Amos 'n' Andy

    Broadway Is My Beat

    The Bob Hope Show

    The Edgar Bergen – Charley McCarthy Show
       (*The Chase and Sanborn Hour*)

Film

Actor

1939: *Another Thin Man*
1941: *Tall, Dark and
      Handsome*
1941: *Private Nurse*
1941: *Buy Me That Town*
1941: *Weekend in Havana*
1941: *Rise and Shine*
1942: *Born to Sing*
1942: *Tortilla Flat*
1942: *Pierre of the Plains*
1942: *Street of Chance*
1943: *Lucky Jordan*
1943: *Taxi Mister*
1943: *Hit the Ice*
1944: *Uncertain Glory*
1944: *To Have and Have Not*
1944: *The Falcon in
      Hollywood*
1945: *Zombies on Broadway*
1945: *Crime Incorporated*
1945: *Why Girls Leave Home*
1945: *Radio Stars on Parade*
1945: *River Gang*
1945: *Captain Kidd*
1945: *Frontier Gal*

1946: *Her Kind of Man*
1946: *Somewhere in the Night*
1946: *The Last Crooked Mile*
1946: *Decoy*
1946: *It's a Wonderful Life*
1947: *Sinbad the Sailor*
1947: *Violence*
1947: *The Gangster*
1948: *Open Secret*
1948: *If You Knew Susie*
1949: *My Dream is Yours*
1949: *Take One False Step*
1950: *The Iroquois Trail*
1951: *Abbott and Costello
      Meet The Invisible Man*
1951: *Behave Yourself*
1951: *Come Fill the Cup*
1952: *Young Man With Ideas*
1952: *Stop You're Killing Me*
1954: *The Diamond Queen*
1954: *Money From Home*
1955: *Guys and Dolls*
1961: *Pocketful of Miracles*

Television

1953 (ABC): *The Jewelers' Showcase (Showcase Theatre)* – Writer and/or Director, various episodes

1953-1957 (ABC) 1957-1964 (CBS): *The Danny Thomas Show (Make Room for Daddy)* – Executive Producer, and/or Producer – Director and/or writer, various episodes.

1954: (CBS): *Lassie* – co-Executive Producer, Director, pilot and early episodes

1954 (NBC): *The Duke* – Actor

1955-56 (CBS): *Damon Runyan Theatre* – Writer and/or Director, various episodes

1957 (ABC): *The Real McCoys* – co-Executive Producer, Director, pilot and early episodes

1960-1968 (CBS): *The Andy Griffith Show* – Executive Producer – Director, various episodes

1961-1966 (CBS): *The Dick Van Dyke Show* – Executive Producer – Director, various episodes

1964-1970 (CBS): *Gomer Pyle, U.S.M.C.* Executive Producer

1965-1968 (NBC): *I Spy* – Creator, Executive Producer – Director, various episodes

1967 (CBS): *Good Morning World* – Executive Producer – Director, pilot and early episodes)

1969 (NBC): *My Friend Tony* – Executive Producer – Director, various episodes

1969 (NBC): *From a Bird's Eye View* – Executive Producer

1969-1970 (NBC): *My World and Welcome To It* – Executive Producer – Director, various episodes

1971 (NBC): *Shirley's World* – Executive Producer

1975 (CBS): *Big Eddie* – Actor

1993 (CBS): *I Spy Returns* – Executive Producer

Index